INTERNATIONAL BACCA

THEORY OF KNOWLEDGE
THE ESSENTIALS

Michael Woolman

Copyright ©IBID Press, Victoria.

www.ibid.com.au

First published in 2011 by IBID Press, Victoria.

Library Catalogue:

Woolman, M.

1. Theory of Knowledge

2. International Baccalaureate.

Series Title: International Baccalaureate in Detail

ISBN: 978 1 921917 08 0

Cover Picture: NEWTON by Eduardo Paolozzi - concourse of the British Library, London, UK.

Frontispiece: Public building at Saltaire, Yorkshire, UK. The town's founder, Sir Titus Salt, believed in providing educational facilities, schools and libraries for his workforce. Saltaire is a UNESCO World Heritage Site in honour of his vision.

This material has been developed independently by the publisher and the content is in no way connected with nor endorsed by the International Baccalaureate Organization.

All copyright statements, refer to the subject guide published by the International Baccalaureate Organization.

IBID Press express their thanks to the International Baccalaureate Organization for permission to reproduce its intellectual property.

Cover design by Key-Strokes.

Published by IBID Press, 36 Quail Crescent, Melton, 3337, Australia.

Printed by KHL Printing.

Preface

Since I wrote the first TOK textbook, *Ways of Knowing*, more than ten years ago, I have visited many IB Diploma schools and worked with TOK teachers and their students and marked several thousand TOK prescribed essays. Over these years it has become clear to me that teachers and students need a TOK text book that explains, in a straightforward manner, the concepts and issues at the heart of the subject and how these concepts and issues interact. So here it is.

The book is divided into three parts.

The first part, *What TOK is About*, briefly describes the origins and purpose of TOK. If you understand the origins and purpose of TOK you will understand the relevance of it to the Diploma as a whole and how it enables you to examine critically the knowledge you are expected to master in your six chosen hexagon subjects. Because the TOK diagram is at the core of the programme the implications and connections within it are explored, and the connections between the diagram and prescribed titles established.

Part Two, *TOK Content*, examines the major concepts in the TOK diagram and the Curriculum Guide. *Ways of Knowing* and *Areas of Knowledge* are explained, as are the eleven linking question concepts. Knowledge Issues, an understanding of which is essential for assessment success, are explained and identified.

Part Three looks at *Assessment*. The importance of identifying knowledge issues in both the Essay and the Presentation is emphasised and the significance of the examiner's annual subject report is stressed.

Throughout the book I have capitalised both Ways of Knowing and Areas of Knowledge to emphasise these are specific TOK concepts used in a TOK context.

This book is a no-nonsense guide to TOK. It provides information about the concepts embedded in the TOK diagram and about the Curriculum Guides linking question concepts and how they both relate to create an awareness of the nature of knowledge that is the IB Diploma's Theory Of Knowledge. It is not, as one colleague called it *TOK for Dummies*. It is TOK for thinking intelligent students and teachers who have limited time at their disposal.

Michael Woolman

Coudrée France 2011

Contents

Part One: What TOK is about

Part Two: TOK Content

Ways of Knowing.

Areas of Knowledge

Linking question concepts

Part Three: Assessment

Chapter 1

The origins and purpose of TOK

Theory of Knowledge (TOK) is unique to the IB Diploma. No other secondary or high school curriculum has anything like it. It is claimed in the Theory of Knowledge Curriculum Guide that TOK is 'a flagship element' of the Diploma Programme

The first thing you as a student, obliged to 'do' TOK, should ask yourself is, 'What is this flagship I have to spend 100 hours of classroom and study time on? At the end of that time I have to write an essay and make a presentation. And, if I don't complete those two assignments I will be denied my diploma even if I have completed all the other requirements. What's so special about TOK? No other secondary or high school programmes include it so why should this one?'

Let's go back a bit. To the swinging 60s when the creative Beatles sung and plucked their way to fame and fortune, and Elvis rocked his hips at the establishment. The creative founding fathers and mothers of the IB Diploma wanted to create a senior school programme providing a sound, liberal education which would guarantee their sons and daughters entry into the world's leading universities. To begin to be educated, these founding parents claimed, our children should be exposed to the two great traditions of learning, the humanities and the sciences. In order for the Diploma to guarantee this, they further argued, it must have certain compulsory elements.

To guarantee you an introduction to understanding the *humanities* they decided on four compulsory subjects

- knowledge of your own language and the ability to communicate with it and share its literature,

- a working knowledge of at least one language other than your own ,

- awareness of the nature of humans as both individuals and as part of the societies they create,

- an understanding of the arts.

For the *sciences* they decided two compulsory subjects were needed:

- you should be aware of the nature of the physical sciences and how these sciences explore the

  non-human aspects of the phenomena of the natural world,

- you should be numerate and aware of mathematical processes .

To begin to be an educated person, they argued, you have to have been introduced to all these six subjects. Even if you found one or more of them challenging that was not a reason why you should give it up. Indeed, some argued, that was a reason for continuing to study it. So they invented the Diploma hexagon.

But it was not enough, these founding mothers and fathers argued, that you be exposed to aspects of the two great traditions of learning, the humanities and the sciences, embedded in the hexagon.

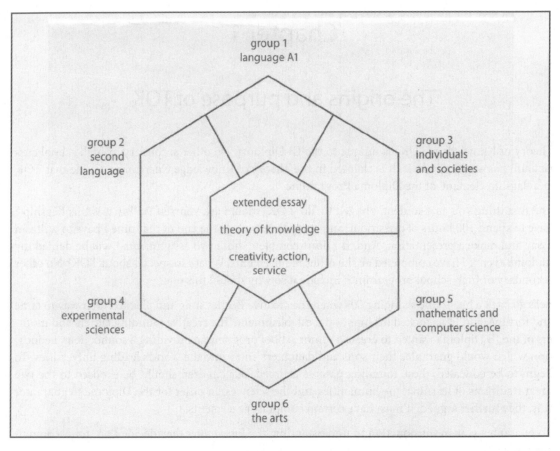

The Diploma hexagon.

You should also know *why* you are being exposed to them. They wanted you to be aware of the differences in the knowledge you were exposed to, why it was important to be grounded in both the humanities and the sciences. They wanted you to understand that the knowledge you use when learning and applying Pythagoras' theorem (Group 5 knowledge) is different from the knowledge you use when learning and responding to a poem by Rabindranath Tagore(Group 6 knowledge). They wanted you to understand knowledge created by a historian (Group 3 knowledge) is different from knowledge created by a scientist (Group 4 knowledge). By becoming aware of the different ways in which knowledge is created, they reasoned, you can begin to think critically about the validity of the types of knowledge you are being exposed to and to understand that the nature of knowledge varies from subject to subject.

Those founding parents wanted to be sure not only that you had a sound liberal education but also that you understood the variety and nature of the different kinds of knowledge to which you were being introduced. Above all they wanted you to examine critically the truth and validity of that knowledge. As you know already they were a creative lot, those founding mothers and fathers, living in a creative time. So they invented TOK.

And that's why you have to spend 100 hours studying TOK and you have to prove, through an essay and a presentation, that you are critically aware of the truth and validity of the knowledge you are acquiring when you study for the IB Diploma.

Chapter 2

The TOK Diagram

The TOK diagram from the Guide[1] introduces the main TOK concepts and their relationships. It is suggested in the Guide that teachers and students may find it useful as a pictorial representation of the course.

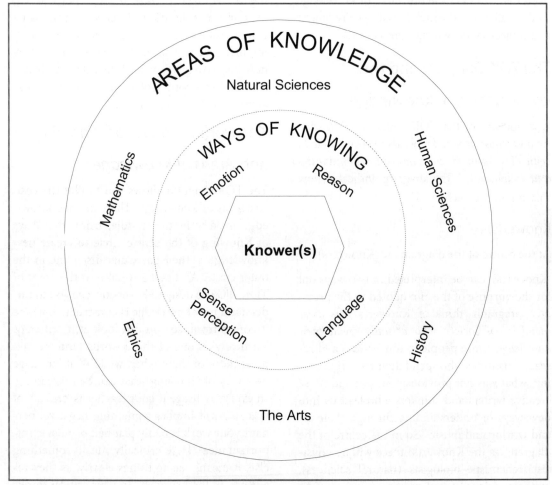

The TOK Diagram

If you look at the *Areas of Knowledge* in the outer circle you can see their relationship to the hexagon.

---

1   2008 ToK Guide Page 6

At the top are *Natural Sciences* which correspond to the 'experimental sciences' of the hexagon and just to the left is *Mathematics*, Group 5. On the right we have *Human Sciences* and *History* which are components of what the hexagon calls 'individuals and societies'. Below them there is the *Arts*. So in that outer circle of the TOK diagram four of the hexagon groups are represented. *Language*, (groups 1 and 2,) is in the inner circle. That leaves *Ethics*, which really is part of the 'individuals and societies', group 3 of the hexagon. (No doubt you will have noticed that Ethics is the only area of knowledge in the outer circle, which is not usually taught as a subject in its own right in schools).

The TOK Diagram and the construction of knowledge

A major aim of the TOK course is *to develop an awareness of how knowledge is constructed , critically examined and renewed by communities and individuals.*[2] The diagram indicates how this aim may be achieved.

Knower(s)

At the centre of the diagram are 'Knower(s)'.

'Knower(s)' can be interpreted in two ways but for the purpose of the aim quoted in the previous paragraph think of 'Knower(s)' as *those members of society who actually create new knowledge*: those people in universities and research institutes who spend their lives discovering what was not previously known and those creative writers and thinkers who lead us into new ways of understanding through their art and writing and music. So in the centre of the diagram, as the Knower(s) there will be physicists, chemists, biologists (natural sciences), mathematicians (mathematics), economists, sociologists, and anthropologists (human sciences); there will be historians (history) and moral philosophers (ethics) and there will be artists (the arts).

According to the TOK diagram these 'Knower(s)' will use the *Ways of Knowing* of the middle circle to create new knowledge in their disciplines (the outer circle). So, it is implied, an astrophysicist will use a combination of these *Ways of Knowing*—reason, sense perception, language and emotion—to find out more about say, a newly observed galaxy. An historian writing a history of the Pinochet years in Chile will also use these *Ways of Knowing* to describe and analyse these Pinochet years, and a mathematician will use these Ways of Knowing to investigate number theory. They will not, of course, use the *Ways of Knowing* in the same combinations. To what extent does a physicist, for instance, use sense perception in creating new knowledge? To what extent does an historian use emotion? Does a mathematician use anything other than reason?

Knower(s)—*Ways of Knowing* and *Areas of Knowledge*

The TOK diagram allows you to plot the construction of knowledge. There are the knowledge makers in the middle, using the Ways of Knowing of the centre circle to create new knowledge in their particular discipline in the outer circle. And that is what is at the heart of TOK. TOK is designed to encourage you to understand how knowledge is constructed, where it comes from, so you can look at it critically. 'Critically' is one of those words (and we will meet more of them when we look at language as a Way of Knowing) that can be misleading. In everyday usage if your teacher is 'critical' of your work it implies something negative, perhaps your work is badly planned or misses important ideas. Here 'critically' means something else, it means seeing things clearly, as they really are, in their context. So your critical thinking about, for instance a new sculpture, will be influenced by the ideas you are introduced to in TOK about the nature of artistic knowledge. To what extent is artistic knowledge to be judged by reason or sense perception or emotion or language? Your critical thinking of the nature of calculus will be enhanced by your TOK awareness of how knowledge in mathematics is created by a combination of reason, sense perception, emotion and/or language.

As its name implies, TOK is about the nature of knowledge. The course encourages you to understand that schools and universities transmit and create a variety of Areas of Knowledge. Each of these areas has its own different truths and justifications. By the end of the course you should begin to understand these different truths and justifications and begin to evaluate these Areas of Knowledge by their own standards.

So that's why those contemporaries of the Beatles, those IB founding fathers and mothers, invented TOK. Their invention is not perfect. Since the 1960s the 'great tradition' of sciences and humanities has been blurred by an ever-increasing attempt by social scientists to model their research on the methods of natural science. The six Areas of Knowledge of the outer ring of the TOK diagram are a selection. The four Ways of Knowing are also a selection. With a little thought you can probably add to both the Areas of Knowledge and the Ways of Knowing. But TOK is a practical construct; a programme designed by concerned educators to help you understand the nature of the knowledge you are studying.

A Caution: The student, as 'Knower'

The TOK diagram in the Curriculum Guide has Knower(s) at the centre. Immediately beneath the diagram are two statements:

- Teachers and students may find figure 1 useful as a pictorial representation of the TOK course.

- Because the course is centred on student reflection and questioning the diagram places the knower(s) as individuals and groups, at the centre.

The suggestion here is the way that you as a student 'know' something, through reflection and questioning, is the same as the way academics and researchers and the creators of knowledge know something, through the *Ways of Knowing* and *Areas of Knowledge*. It might seem the diagram and the two statements together suggest your learning, your becoming a 'knower', is itself similar to the process with which academics, researchers and artists create new knowledge.

On the surface this idea may seem plausible. Of course you use sense perception, reason, language and emotion *to learn*. You use your eyes to read text books and literature, your ears to listen to your teachers and your other senses to become familiar with how thing feel, taste and smell. You use reason to check out what you have read or heard. It is with language, through reading and listening that you acquire most of your learning, your knowing, at school. And you use your emotions to understand ideas and concepts, and respond to what you learn.

But the *learned* knowledge you acquire at school is not the same kind of knowledge as the knowledge constructed by the research Knower(s). You do not construct new knowledge. What you do is process existing knowledge, making it meaningful for yourself. When you are introduced to Pythagoras Theorem it might be that your teacher sets up a situation in which you 'discover' the sum of the areas of the squares on two sides of a right angle triangle are equal to the area of square on the hypotenuse. But although that 'discovery' might help you to understand the theorem it is not knowledge you have created. You may, as the teachers might say, have 'constructed' that knowledge. You constructed it because it was put before you in such a way that the reconstruction of what other people have known for two thousand years was possible.

Most of what you learn at school is what is known as 'knowledge by authority'. To understand this it is worth looking briefly at two school subjects: natural science and history. In school science students undertake identical, or similar investigations, all of which have been undertaken before, under the direction of a teacher, with an outcome that is predictable and examinable for the purpose of proving you have understood it. In contrast 'real' science probes for new knowledge seeking understanding as yet unknown. This does not mean that school science has no value. It demands careful observation, rational interpretation, precise use of language and a search for truth. School history is similar: it demands careful analysis and a search for truth, but it is not real history. It is packaged. Students work with material given to them. Original sources are not available (although facsimiles might be) and because school history is assessed by examinations, students must predict what the examiner wants and deliver accordingly.

In normal classroom activities the student as 'knower' at the centre of the TOK diagram is quite a different 'Knower' from the researcher as a Knower. Your Extended Essay, however, with its demand for original research takes you, however briefly, into the world of the researcher as Knower. Here you are expected to produce a little original research, to creatively extend the boundaries of knowledge, be it however small an extension, to find out, to construct, something no-one has found out or constructed and to come to a conclusion nobody has ever reached before. At that point you, as a Knower, come to the centre of the diagram with the same status as the established researcher.

Assessment and TOK Diagram

'OK'. I can hear you saying. 'The idea that TOK was born out of educational idealism may be all well and fine but the real curriculum of any exam subject can be only really seen in the exam questions. When you prepare for an exam you look carefully at past papers. What do the TOK exam papers tell us?'

The Prescribed Essay

Well, there are no exam papers in the conventional sense. Each year the IB publishes ten TOK essay titles and students must select one of these and, in their own time, write a 1600 word essay exploring the TOK issues in their selected title. So, to know what TOK is really about look at these titles.

Let's look at some of these essay titles, selected at random for the 2012 list and see how they relate to the TOK diagram.

Here is question 3:

Using history and at least one other area of knowledge, examine the claim that it is possible to attain knowledge despite problems of bias and selection.

The relationship of this question to the TOK diagram is obvious. What the student is expected to do is look critically at how Ways of Knowing-reason, perception, emotion and language—are used by historians and how these Ways of Knowing create problems of bias and selection, and then compare this with how the same Ways of Knowing with emphasis on bias and selection in another Area of Knowledge, the Arts perhaps or natural or human science.

Here is question 10:

Through different methods of justification, we can reach conclusions in ethics that are as well supported as those provided in mathematics. To what extent would you agree?

Once again the relationship of the question to the TOK diagram is clear. Ethics and mathematics are the *Areas of Knowledge* and students are expected to explore the ways in which *justification* is a key process ethicists and mathematicians use to create knowledge in their disciplines. Of course, being a TOK question students are expected to show how the *Ways of Knowing*—reason, sense perception, language and emotion—can be regarded as generating justification.

In both of these essay titles the initial focus is on the *Areas of Knowledge*. In some essay titles the initial focus is on the *Ways of Knowing*.

Here is question 1:

Knowledge is generated through the interaction of critical and creative thinking. Evaluate this statement in two areas of knowledge.

Although the phrase *'Ways of Knowing'* is not specifically stated students are expected to relate 'critical and creative thinking' to *Ways of*

Knowing, asking themselves in what ways reason, language, emotion and sense perception generate critical and creative thinking and to apply their ideas to two *Areas of Knowledge*.

Another example of focussing initially on *Ways of Knowing* is in Question 2:

Compare and contrast knowledge, which can be expressed in words/symbols, with knowledge that cannot be expressed in this way. Consider Creativy, action, service (CAS) and one or more areas of knowledge.

Knowledge, which can be expressed (or not expressed) in words and symbols, is clearly an invitation to discuss the advantages and disadvantages of language as a way of knowing. Considering CAS as equivalent to an area of knowledge is an interesting development. Students who choose this title must begin by defining what knowledge had been created in them by their CAS experience. They then need to compare that new personal knowledge with at least one of the *Areas of Knowledge* in the TOK's diagram. In this case the 'Knower(s)' in the middle of the diagram has clearly moved from the academics and researchers to the students undertaking their CAS and analysing what new knowledge their CAS experience has created within themselves.

Linking Question Concepts.

The Diagram introduces the principal concepts of TOK and suggests possible relationships. What it does not indicate are the 11 subsidiary linking concepts, which are introduced in the main body of the Guide. These concepts: Belief, Certainty, Culture, Evidence, Experience, Explanation, Interpretation, Intuition, Technology, Truth, and Values, are also part of TOK and are discussed in chapter 15.

Chapter 3

Knowledge Issues

Here are the stated objectives of the TOK course[1]:

Having followed the TOK course, students should be able to:

- analyse critical knowledge claims, their underlying assumptions and their implications

- generate questions, explanations, conjectures, hypotheses, alternative ideas and possible solutions in response to knowledge issues concerning areas of knowledge, ways of knowing and students' own experience as learners

- demonstrate an understanding of different perspectives on knowledge issues

- draw links and make effective comparisons between different approaches to knowledge issues that derive from areas of knowledge, ways of knowing, theoretical positions and cultural values

- demonstrate an ability to give a personal, self-aware response to a knowledge issue

- formulate and communicate ideas clearly with due regard for accuracy and academic honesty.

The key phrase is *knowledge issues*. There it is, in four of the six objectives. The phrase also appears 43 times in the assessment criteria which the examiners have in front of them when they mark the essays and presentations. 'Knowledge Issues' (KI), is a concept developed specifically for the IB Diploma's TOK Course. Once you understand what is meant by the term and can identify and create your own knowledge issues you will be on the way to mastering TOK.

So, what is a 'knowledge issue'? Here is a simplified version of the IB's own definition:

A knowledge issue is:

- An open ended question

- explicitly about knowledge,

- using TOK concepts (specifically the 4 *Ways of Knowing*, the 6 *Areas of Knowledge* and the 11 linking question concepts)

- suggesting relationships between these concepts. [2]

---

1   2008 ToK Guide page 5
2   Adapted from *Understanding knowledge issues*, on line curriculum document 2009 IBO

On its own this definition may not seem helpful. Perhaps the easiest way to understand knowledge issues is to see how they are used in assessment.

Knowledge Issues and Assessment

TOK is formally assessed by an essay (40 marks) on a prescribed title, externally examined, and a presentation (20 marks) marked internally by your TOK teacher.

The Essay

You have already seen how the essay you write reflects closely the content of the TOK diagram. It also demands an awareness and understanding of knowledge issues. The essay is marked according to four criteria, the first three of which are focussed entirely on knowledge issues. (The fourth criterion evaluates how well you have structured and written the essay.) Here are these first three criteria:

Criterion A.
Understanding *knowledge issues*.

To score well in this you have to identify the *knowledge issues* implicit in the title you have selected and to show an understanding of these *issues*.

Criterion B.
Knower's perspective

To score well you have to connect the *knowledge issues* you have identified to your own personal experience as a learner, to show a 'personal and reflective exploration' of the *knowledge issues*.

Criterion C.
Quality of analysis of *knowledge issues*

To score well the discussion of the *knowledge issues* you identify must be compelling

One of the prescribed titles for May 2009 was *When should we trust our senses to give us truth?* Here are three examples of knowledge issues that the examiner suggests could be addressed in responding to the prescribed essay [3]

3   From the ToK Examiner's Report May 2009

16

- *To what extent do our senses give us the truth?*

- *To what extent do reason, emotion, and language (and other factors) affect our sense perception?*

- *What is the scope and what are the limits of sensory information in different areas of knowledge?*

If you apply the four parts of the definition of a knowledge issue to the first knowledge issue defined above (To what extent do our senses give us the truth?) you will find all four parts are a good fit.

Is it open-ended?

Yes, clearly it is. An open-ended questions is one which doesn't limit the respondent in the range of his or her answer. This question invites open-ended discussion of how realizable (how truthful?) is sense perception and what is meant by 'truth' in different *Areas of Knowledge*.

- Is it specifically about knowledge?

Yes, it certainly is.

The obvious way forward with this question is to look at what 'truth' sense perception gives us when creating knowledge in several *Areas of Knowledge*, comparing 'truth' in mathematics say with 'truth' in the arts or the natural sciences. So, yes, it is specifically about knowledge.

- Does it use TOK concepts?

Yes, it does. 'Senses' is clearly to be taken as the sense perception and 'truth' is one of the 11 linking question concepts.

- Does it suggest a relationship between these concepts?

Yes again, it clearly does, and that relationship between truth and sense perception will be the subject matter of that essay.

Pause for a moment and ask yourself the same four questions about the two further examples of knowledge issues from the same Examiner's Report. You will see they too fit the description given above.

- *To what extent do reason, emotion, and language (and other factors) affect our sense perception?*

- *What is the scope and what are the limits of sensory information in different areas of knowledge?*

Often the essay question is a knowledge issue in itself and to explore the issue means generating more knowledge issues, sometimes a little more narrow in their focus than the initial question.

The Presentation

In the presentation you have to ' identify and explore the knowledge issues' implicit in a real life situation of your own choosing.

Here are some examples of knowledge issues (again from the 2009 Examiner's Report) The TOK terms have been italicised.

- Real life situation:
  The bombing of Coventry in the United Kingdom in World War Two.

Knowledge Issue:
To what extent can we use *reason* to evaluate two competing *ethical* systems?

- Real life situation:
  The inauguration of the Large Hadron Collider in Switzerland

Knowledge Issue:
What is the scope of the *scientific* method in attempting to establish *truths*?

- Real life situation:
  The death of Bogon —the last speaker of the Kasabe language in Cameroon

Knowledge Issue:
In what ways does *language* affect how we *interpret* the world?

- Real life situation:
  President Ahmadinejad of Iran calls for a conference to establish whether the Jewish Holocaust ever happened.

Knowledge Issue:
How can we draw a clear line between fact and *interpretation* in *history*?

The bombing of Coventry in World War II is an opportunity to discuss the part *reason* (a Way of Knowing) plays in the creation of ethical (an Area of Knowledge) ideas? The inauguration of the Hadron Collider is clearly an invitation to look at natural science as an Area of Knowledge and to discuss what natural scientists regard as truth. When considering knowledge issues the concepts and connections, and the language of the TOK diagram are always near the surface.

Chapter 4

Ways of Knowing1: Reason

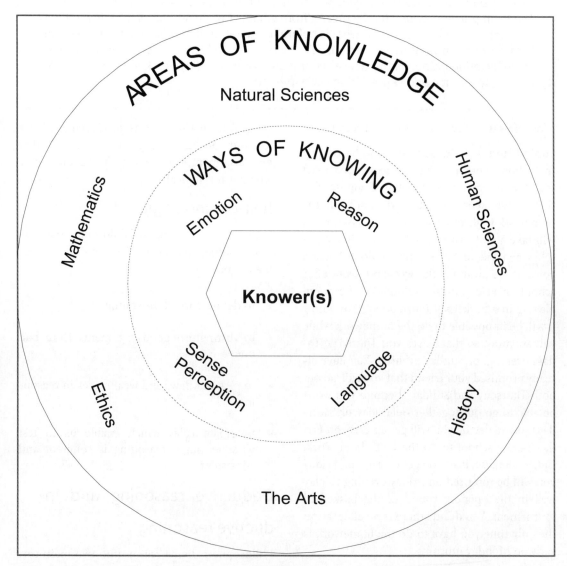

ToK Diagram

Reason is one of the four *Ways of Knowing* in the centre circle of the TOK diagram. There are 21 questions under 'Reason' in the TOK Guide. In the prescribed essay titles the word 'reason' occurs frequently. One 2011 title is simply *Compare the roles of language and reason in history.* It is also implicit in questions that mention *Ways of Knowing: How can the different Ways of Knowing help us to distinguish between something that is true and something that is believed to be true?* Reason is one of the *Ways of Knowing* you have to consider when responding to this question. Reason is at the heart of TOK.

> ### Reason/ Rationalism
>
> Rationalism is the doctrine or theory that reason rather than experience is the foundation for certainty in knowledge. Rationalists argue that experience can not be trusted and therefore, can give no sound basis for knowledge. If we can know anything at all, rationalists claim, it is because we have reflected rationally upon it. This 'rational' knowledge is called *a priori* knowledge, knowledge that is created by reasoning and reasoning only. The Latin phrase *a priori* literally means 'from what is before' so rationalist knowledge is knowledge which comes 'from what is before' in our rational minds. Rationalists develop knowledge from what they claim are self-evident facts, which are *a priori*, and which we know by rationalising. Mathematical axioms are examples of *a priori* knowledge. You can read more about *a priori* knowledge in Chapter 10.

Most of us use of reason in our everyday lives.

Suppose today is Thursday and you have some math homework that has to be handed in at the start of school on Monday. Suppose also that you are keen on math and want to do the homework well. You also know the assignment will take about two hours. Now, you ask yourself, when will be the best time to do it? You are going to be away for the weekend, from after school on Friday until late Sunday afternoon, playing in a basketball tournament. You know it will be impossible to do the homework while you are away, so that leaves you Thursday (today) evening, or Sunday evening. You have already promised your friend that you will go out both Thursday and Sunday (because you won't be able to go out together on Friday or Saturday) so you decide you will get up early on Friday, before school to do the math homework. But, you realise, if you do get up early on Friday you will be too tired on Friday evening to play well in the opening round of the basketball tournament. You decide there is no alternative: the only time you have to do the homework is early on Monday morning.

This is clearly an example of your reasoning, your logical thinking. You have a problem: when to do your homework. You ask yourself what are the possible solutions to the problem. You consider each solution and finally conclude there is only one time to do the work and that is early on Monday morning. You define a problem, consider solutions, and come to a conclusion. Your reasoning has produced evidence for your conclusion. Logic determines whether your argument, your reasoning, is good or bad, whether it is logical.

Reason and Logic

Logic is the branch of philosophy that explores some, not all, of the ways we reason. It attempts:

- to define 'correct' reasoning

- to distinguish good arguments from bad ones

- to pick out flaws and weaknesses in reasoning

- to create rules which enable us to test whether our reasoning is coherent and consistent.

Deductive reasoning and inductive reasoning.

Philosophers divide reason into two main categories, *formal reasoning,* known as 'deductive logic' (logic is the name of the branch of philosophy that deals with reasoning) and *informal reasoning,* known as 'inductive logic'. Natural and human scientists, mathematicians, historians and scholars from all disciplines use both formal and informal reasoning to present their arguments and to justify their claims to know.

Reason is the mental faculty to draw conclusions from evidence. When a historian makes a claim to know why the Great Wall of China was built it is expected he or she will provide the reasons for this claim. These reasons must be coherent, consistent with the evidence and logical.

Deductive Logic

Deductive logic is concerned with the rules for determining when an argument is valid. It structures arguments in a formal way to help us understand, as clearly as possible, the reasoning behind the arguments. It does not concern itself with truth at all, only with the process of reasoning. Deductive logic produces knowledge based on reason rather than experience.

Reduced to simple deductive logic your 'homework' argument goes like this:

I have to hand in my math homework on Monday.
The only time I can do it well is early Monday morning.
Therefore I will do it early on Monday morning.

(This simplified argument omits some implied premises and conclusions which we will return to later.)

Consider this argument:
Caitriona is an 11th grade student at The International School of Uganda (ISU).
All 11th grade students at ISU study taxidermy.
Therefore Caitriona studies taxidermy.

This is a valid argument. If all the 11th grade students at ISU study taxidermy, and Caitriona is an 11th grade student at ISU then she must study taxidermy. Notice the argument does not have to be true to be valid. Nobody at ISU studies taxidermy but the argument is valid because the conclusions follow from the premises. The premises can be false but the argument is valid. Deductive logic tests reasoning, not truth.

In the language of logic these three line arguments are called syllogisms. Each of the first two lines is called a premise. The last line is called the conclusion. The three sentences together contain an argument. If the conclusion follows logically from the two premises the argument is said to be valid. If the conclusion does not follow logically from the premises it is invalid.

Arguments like this are known as deductive arguments. Whether a deductive argument is valid or invalid depends on whether its form is valid. Here is a simple deductive argument that, despite its obvious lack of truth, is valid

All 11th grade students are clever.
Frank's dog is an 11th grade student.
Therefore Frank's dog is clever.

This is clearly a valid argument even though its premises, (the second one certainly, the first you decide) are not true.

Of course most arguments are more complex than this. Very few 'real life' arguments can be reduced to two premises and a conclusion. Look again at your homework argument.

I have to hand in my math homework on Monday.
The only time I can do it well is early Monday morning.
Therefore: I will do it early on Monday morning.

This is your argument reduced to its basic form. The full argument is much more complex. Some intermediate premises and their conclusions have been omitted because it is assumed they are taken for granted or implied. Recall how your argument was developed. You know the homework will take two hours and you want to do it well. An intermediate conclusion could be inserted between the first and second premise.
I want to do my homework wellIt will take me two hours to do it well. Therefore I must find two hours when I can do it.

But this addition does not cover all your reasoning. You have not given the reasons why you cannot do it at other times.

From Friday after school until late Sunday afternoon I am away playing basketball.
On Thursday evening and Sunday evening I have promised to go out.

Therefore the only time left is early Friday or early Monday.

Even this is not the full argument.

I want to play well in the basketball tournament.
If I do my homework early on Friday I will be too tired to play well on Friday evening.
Therefore I must not do it on Friday morning.

The complete argument is now:
Premise 1. *I have to hand in my math homework on Monday.*
Premise 2. *I want to do my homework well.*
Premise 3. *It will take me two hours to do it well.*
Intermediate Conclusion One:
Therefore I must find two hours when I can do it.

Premise 4. *From Friday after school until late Sunday afternoon I am away playing basketball.*
Premise 5. *On Thursday evening and Sunday evening I have promised to go out.*
Intermediate Conclusion Two:
Therefore the only time left is early Friday or early Monday.

Premise 6. *I want to play well in the basketball tournament.*
Premise 7. *If I do my homework early on Friday I will be too tired to play well on Friday evening.*
Intermediate Conclusion Three:
Therefore I must not do it on Friday morning.

Premise 8. *The only time I can do it well is early Monday morning.*
Conclusion:

Therefore, I will do it early on Monday morning.

Unless an argument is fully stated in this way, and often arguments in 'real life' are not fully stated, we have to guess what is assumed for the conclusion.

Symbolic deductive logic

Logicians have devised ways of using symbols to depict arguments thus distancing themselves from the potentially ambiguous language of premises and conclusions. Aristotle started this use of symbols when he laid down the rules for the use of the syllogism. Look again at the syllogism about Frank's dog.

All 11th grade students are clever.
Frank's dog is an 11th grade student.
Therefore Frank's dog is clever.

This is what logicians call a 'categorical syllogism'. The premises show that one set of things (a category, hence 'categorical'), in this case Frank' s dog, is either included or excluded from another set of things, here 11th grade students. To distance themselves from emotive words like 'dog' and 'clever' logicians substitute symbols for verbal categories.

All A is B   (All 11th grade students are clever).
All C is A   (Frank's dog is an 11th grade student).
All C is B (Therefore Frank's dog is clever),

No matter the linguistic content of the syllogism any argument in the same form is valid. Any differences may invalidate the conclusion.

Inductive logic

Generalisations and Analogies

Inductive logic is the reasoning we use when we make generalisations or analogies. We use our experience, our empirical knowledge and make inferences from that experience. Therefore, inductive knowledge is fundamentally different from the 'pure' reason of deductive logic. Deductive logic is independent of any sense perception or empiricism. When we use inductive logic the reliability of the empirical evidence, on which we base our conclusions, determines the soundness of the argument.

Inductive Logic 1: Generalisations

If you were asked the following question how would you respond?

Will your next English class be interesting?

You would presumably base your answer on your experience of previous English classes. You would generalise from your experience. If your English classes have always been interesting (and for the sake of this example let us presume they have) it would be normal and rational and obvious for you to say, 'Yes, my next English class will be interesting'. When you make a generalisation like this from your experience, you are using inductive logic. Your experience is gained through your senses, mainly what you see and hear in your English classes, but it could also be, if you have a zany teacher, what you feel, taste and smell. Inductive logic is not concerned with the absolute certainty of an argument. Its two main features are

- it gives good reasons for supporting a conclusion but does not guarantee that conclusion

- its conclusion contains information that is not in the argument.

You can see these features in the answer to the question about your English class. Your reason might be

- in the past my English classes have always been interesting (this is a good reason but not a guarantee)

- therefore, it is likely my next English class will be interesting (this conclusion is not in the argument).

Of course, the 'it is likely' is important here. You cannot be certain your next English class will be interesting. Your teacher might not turn up, you might be given a surprise test which may not be at all interesting, and you may start a new text which you find totally boring. However if your experience to date indicates that you will find the class interesting, then *it is likely* the next class will also be interesting.

But can we cope with that *it is likely*?

What makes your generalisation reliable? Did you make your response on the basis of four previous classes? Or forty? Or four hundred? Have you had a sufficient number of classes on which to base your generalisation? And are the past classes indications of the classes to come? Can you be reasonably sure they will continue to be the same?

Three Tests for Soundness

Inductive reasoning conclusions based on generalisations must be treated with caution. There are three tests of the soundness of the generalisation which you should apply before you accept any knowledge based on generalisations, the tests of Sufficient Number, of Varying Circumstances and of the Exceptions. Take, for example, this generalisation:

In every country's capital city there is an international school

Test One: Sufficient Number.

- on what numerical information is this statement based?

- was it based on information from every country in the world?

- or was it based on information from most of the countries?

- is it a generalisation from a widely travelled educator who has visited many (how many is 'many'?) countries and has found an international school in every capital

- or is it a generalisation from a researcher who has researched 20% percent of the world's capital cities and found they have international schools and therefore inferred that all capital cities have an international school?

- what numerical information would be acceptable as sound evidence for generalisation

Test Two: Varying Circumstances

Is the generalisation based on evidence from all parts of the world or is it localised? It might be the generalisation was made based on the experience of someone living in Japan, who, aware of international schools in the capitals of all the countries near to Japan presumed that every capital city had an international school. Or it may be that the generalisation was made by business people who regularly visit the financial centres of the world and were aware that many of the expatriates with whom they work send their children to international schools. These people are not deliberately given uncertain information but the circumstances on which they base their generalisations are limited.

Test Three: Exceptions

Has a thorough and reliable search for exceptions been made? In the case of international schools in capital cities this would seem to be the most obvious test to start with. Look first at those capitals that are less likely to have an international school than the big international centres.

It might be that after applying these three tests to the generalisation you might change it to read: In almost every country's capital city there is an international school.

In this form the statement is acceptable as inductive logic.

Inductive Logic 2: Analogy

When we reason (or induce) by analogy we compare two things that are similar in some ways and then infer they are similar in other ways too. For example, scientists working with laboratory animals are reasoning analogy when they apply the knowledge they discover about animal physiology to human physiology. They are inferring that because animal and human physiology is similar, the knowledge they construct through animal experimentation will be relevant to humans.

You have probably come across analogies in tests you have done at school. Part of the American College Entrance Scholastic Aptitude Test (SAT) tests your thinking skills and vocabulary through analogies. You are given a pair of words and then have to select, from a given list, words that are similar in their relationship to the given pair.

Consider this example.
ACRE:LAND
        a. distance: space
        b. kinsfolk: family
        c. gallon: liquid
        d. degree: thermometer
        e. year: birthday

You must first decide on the relationship between ACRE and LAND and then decide if any of the other pairs have the same relationship. The answer here is fairly obvious. In the same way an acre is a measure of land a gallon is a measure of liquid. (This is obvious if you know what a gallon is but many people living outside of America measure liquid in litres. This question has a clear cultural bias of which the test maker may not have been aware).

Areas of Knowledge using analogies are ethics (when a given situation may be compared to another where a clear moral principle has been established), economics and history.

Reason and other Ways of Knowing.

Reason is frequently contrasted with sense perception or 'experience' as a *Way of Knowing*. It is also often regarded to be in conflict with conclusions based partly on other (non TOK) *Ways of Knowing* such as, memory, authority, faith and superstition. Of course conclusions in ways of knowing may involve some degree of reasoning.

Can logic create knowledge?

The answer to this question, according to Dr Aidan Seery, the author of *The Limits of Logic* is a firm 'no'.

The Limits of Logic

(or Would Mr Spock have enjoyed meeting Euclid?)

Despite the fact that this question explores the nature of logic so embedded in the notion of Mr Spock, this is a question that few Trekkies have asked. To answer they would have to look briefly at the history of logic.

The ability to reason is often cited as the distinguishing characteristic of the human species. Logic began with attempts to bring some rules to this ability. The Greeks discovered common patterns that underpin reasoning. These patterns they defined with 'laws'. Aristotle formulated these laws, or arguments, in the realm of real language,and Euclid formulated them in geometry. Over two thousand years after Euclid the great German philosopher Kant (1724-1803) used Euclid's geometry to defend his revolutionary theory about the nature of mind and reasoning. Many thinkers of Kant's time dismissed the thought that there might be many different kinds of points and lines in the one reality. Euclid was seen not only as the epitome of logical thought but also as being the source of the only and final description of true nature and reality.

The beginning of the demise of Euclidean geometry and with it the greatly influential theory of reasoning of Kant can be traced to a Jesuit mathematician named Saccheri, who predates Kant by several years. Saccheri, ironically, set himself the task of freeing Euclid, once and for all, from any doubt of flaw. To do this he made use of one of Aristotle's rules of logic: if you assume the opposite of a rule, and work with it, you should encounter a contradiction. This is sound logic! So Saccheri systematically worked out Euclid's propositions, one after another, while assuming that one of them was false. (The one he chose to assume was false was the fifth postulate: parallel lines only meet at infinity). He was rather disconcerted after thirty years when he had still not come across a clear contradiction. However, having decided he was almost sure of a contradiction, he decided to publish his results. The title of his book was understandably Euclid Freed From Every Flaw. He then died. Sadly he died without being aware of his immense achievement. Contrary to proving geometry could not work without the five postulates of Euclid, he had developed what is now known as non- Euclidean geometry.

The story of Saccheri's disconcertment and his search for a preconceived conclusion suggests three things.

Firstly, and most importantly, the connection between logical structure and reality was questioned and this opened up the possibility of other forms of seeing and dealing with reality. The twentieth century debate on how to interpret the Quantum Mechanics pivoted on the adequacy of our logic to deal with the phenomena and theoretical constructs the physicists had developed.

Secondly, reasoning, while adhering to patterns that are as stable as rules does not guarantee the conclusion is understood. Saccheri did not understand where his conclusion was leading. If logic is only concerned with the structure of an argument, then it is clear that nothing can be learned from a conclusion. Thus logic does not lead to knowledge. I can produce a perfect line of argument that either Euclid or Spock would be proud of and nevertheless I may not understand the consequences of the conclusion.

Thirdly, even if the conclusion is reached by means of absolutely meticulous logical deduction, it can still be rejected because of deep prejudice. Saccheri not only did not realise the consequences of the argument he developed, he went further and claimed what he had discovered reinforced the thesis he had set out to prove: Euclid's geometry was free of flaws. Now it is one thing not to have understood the significance of an argument but it is more serious to then take the argument and use it in a way that twists the conclusion to one's own purpose. It is to be assumed that someone who spent thirty years attempting to prove Euclid was right was either fanatically devoted to him or passionately interested in the truth. After some research I believe the latter to be true. What can be deduced from the story is our prejudices and cultural imprisonment can dominate our thinking

We have seen what logic is not: it is not a source of knowledge; it is not a picture of reality; it is not a defence against prejudice or cultural boundedness.

So what is it? The answer is embedded in the notion of Mr Spock.
Observe him.

Firstly, he almost never takes the initiative: he is the watchdog over arguments that could be fallacious and therefore plays a reactive role. He points out irrelevant arguments but rarely adds a creative one.

Secondly, his picture of reality is very different from Aristotle's reality, or indeed from our own. His logic has nothing to do with a particular reality.

Thirdly, Spock is for the most part cultureless, or perhaps his culture is the culture of logic and thus not in conflict with it. (Even when the Enterprise seeks the supposedly dead Spock we get no sense of Vulcan culture). Thus Spock is fortunate (or unfortunate?) as his logic is not culturally distorted.

We have seen what logic is not. Let's end with what it is. In the form of a syllogism of course.

Logic enables us to recognise fallacies.

Fallacies occur in arguments that are at the centre of a theory of knowledge

Therefore logic lies at the centre of knowledge

And would Spock have enjoyed meeting Euclid? They would both have agreed on the need to avoid fallacious arguments but Euclid would not have understood Spock's concepts of space and reality. To what extent Euclid was something other than a logical egghead we cannot be sure. Does Mr Spock enjoy meeting anyone? Certainly he would not have had much respect for Saccheri's misplaced search for truth.

Chapter 5

Ways of Knowing 2: Sense Perception

At any one moment our senses are gathering vast amounts of information. As you read this, your senses, as well as telling you what you are reading and where you are reading it, are telling you who else is in the room, what colour the walls are, the temperature, the brightness of the light that is enabling you to see the page, and that the clock in the corner is ticking. And, a myriad of other things you can list if you allow yourself to be aware of these sensations.

Sense threshold

What we can actually sense depends on what psychologists call our *sense threshold*. Different animals have different thresholds. A tracker dog's sense of smell is quite different from a human's sense of smell and there is even a great difference between the sense of smell of different humans.

In a crowded room with lots of people speaking I find it very difficult to converse with the one or two people nearby. What I have to do is filter out all that background noise and concentrate on what is being said in my small group. This is known as 'signal detection' and when I do this I am trying to minimize all the sounds other than those coming from my group. I am deliberately trying to filter the sensations I am receiving.

You know a candle flame will be extinguished if you cover the burning candle with a glass jar. You know this because you have used one of your senses—sight—and seen it happen. The most obvious way we know anything is through our senses. They connect us to our environment through touch, taste, sight, smell and sound.

Our brains, the physical organs through which we 'know' everything, are insulated from the 'real world' by our skulls, strong walls of bone. We can receive knowledge into our brains only through the connections that link the brain to the 'real world'.

These connections are linked to:

- our eyes— respond to wavelengths of electromagnetic radiation or 'light'

- our ears— respond to changes in air pressure or 'sound'

- our noses— respond to chemicals or 'smell'

- our skin— senses change in temperature and humidity or 'tactility'.

- our tongues— respond to chemicals through groups of cells called taste buds.

The sensations of light, sound, smell, taste and tactility are turned into nerve impulses, or messages. These impulses, or messages, are the only information the brain receives. The brain itself has no direct contact with the outside world. Using the impulses our brains create the 'real world' inside our skulls. We do not see, hear, smell, feel or taste anything until our brains have interpreted the signals we get from our senses. A simple analogy is that of an insulated underground bunker following a nuclear explosion. Any people in the bunker (the brain) can receive information only through any sensors they may have available to them. They may have temperature and radioactivity sensors and video cameras monitoring the outside world, but they do not have direct access to that world. The information they have is only that which the sensors give them, plus their experience in interpreting that information.

Perception

But, 'knowing' through our senses isn't just being aware of the sensations bombarding us. Our brains don't just receive signals, they interpret them and place the signals in the context of everything they already know. Our brains are programmed to do this automatically.

Because our brains continually interpret the sense data they receive, some psychologists and philosophers claim that the old adage

Seeing is Believing.....
should really be.....
Believing is Seeing.

Empirical Knowledge.

Knowledge that we obtain through our senses is called empirical knowledge.

The word *empirical* comes from the name of Sextus Empiricus, a philosopher and physician who lived and worked in Alexandria and Athens in the 3rd century AD. Little is known about him but one of his main works *Against the Professors* is an early *Theory of Knowledge* treatise in which he examines the nature of knowledge in the arts and sciences. In this work he defined the two main principles of what is now known as empiricism:

- One: All knowledge is based on experience that is the experience of the senses.

- Two: The knowledge we acquire through our senses is the basis of understanding, which is the making of that experience meaningful to us.

Hard line empiricists claim that all knowledge must be based on 'the test of experience'. They reject all other ways of knowing. It is not always clear what is meant by 'the test of experience'. A common understanding of the word is 'based on observation and experiment', the former of which is completely sense dependent.

Sense Perception: Some Complications

Beware of what your senses tell you. Or, more accurately, beware of how your brain filters what your senses tell you. Often your brain uses information it already has to interpret what you see, feel, hear, touch and smell. This interpretation can easily distort the 'reality'. Here are some of the ways your brain may filter information from your senses.

- *Through your past experience.*
  Your past experience can often condition you to expect things and we often see or hear what we expect to rather than what really happens.
  What does your past experience tell you is going to happen when you are watching a movie and you hear low, slow, quiet music from the soundtrack?

- *Through social and cultural conditioning.*
  Our prejudices and assumptions often lead us to false conclusions.
  What would you immediately think if a new male teacher came into the room this morning with an unshaven face, three earrings in each ear and wearing a T-shirt on which was written: Shit Happens?

- *Through spatial familiarity.*
  Our brain appears to need to want us to see patterns or shapes with which we are already familiar.
  Most people who look at this two pronged trident try in vain to interpret it as a three dimensional object.

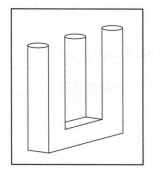

Two-pronged trident

- *Through our biological limitations.*
  Our perception is limited by our biology. Humans can only perceive what their senses and nervous systems allow them to perceive. Some of us can certainly see further and hear more clearly than others, but none of us can see as clearly at night as an owl or hear as keenly as an elephant. What would your 'real' world be if you had the sight of an eagle, the hearing of a dog, or the taste buds of a cow?

- *Through our existing learning structures.*
  The way we perceive the world is influenced by an important part of our conceptual structure: how we use our brains to solve problems or create new knowledge for ourselves. If you are learning a foreign language, you try to use the conceptual structure you have learned from the other languages you already know. If the structure of the new language is different from those you already know you may have difficulties. If, for instance, your known languages are all based on sentence structures that need verbs, and the new language sentences do not need verbs, you may have initial difficulties learning the language.

- *Through seeing what is not there.*
  We cannot explain what happens when we are faced with optical illusions. If something is not there, how can we see it? How can you 'see' plaster mouldings around windows which turn out, on close inspection, to be painted on a flat surface?

- *Through our dependence on language.*
  The labels we use for ideas and objects (our language) influences the way we think (or don't think) about them. Advertisers are aware of the power of 'language' to influence our perception of products. What does the word 'colonial' mean to you?

- *Through filtering.*
  Our senses receive much more information than we are capable of processing. At any one time, we filter out much of the information we are receiving and accept only that which is understandable or of interest.

If you visit China without knowing Chinese, you will not even notice many street signs or directions or advertisements which you cannot understand.

- *Through self-perception.*
  Finally, we have a perception of ourselves. It is different, probably, from the perception others have of us. But it seems likely that how we think of ourselves will influence our perception of ourselves in relationship to others.

Sense Perception

Some comments about perception that you might consider

putting into the context of your own sense perception.

A fool sees not the same tree as a wise man sees.

William Blake

People only see what they are prepared to see.

Ralph Waldo Emerson

Were the eye not attuned to the Sun, the Sun could never be seen by it.

Göethe

What can give us surer knowledge than our senses?

With what else can we distinguish the true from the false?

Lucretius

A rock pile ceases to be a rock pile the moment a single man contemplates it,

bearing within him the image of a cathedral.

Saint-Exupery

All seeing is seeing-as ... There is no 'innocent eye'. Nietzsche

called this the 'fallacy of the immaculate conception'. In order for you to receive some-

thing you must add to your sense datum; you must furnish an element of projection.

R Abel

It seems that the human mind has first to construct forms, independently, before it can find them in things. Knowledge cannot spring from experience alone, but only from the comparisons of the inventions of the intellect with observed fact.

Albert Einstein

Observers are not led by the same physical evidence to the same picture of the universe unless their linguistic backgrounds are similar or can in some way be calibrated.

Benjamin Whorf

The human brain craves understanding. It cannot understand without simplifying; that is without reducing things to a common element. However, all simplifications are arbitrary and lead us to drift insensibly away from reality.

Lecomte du Nou

Chapter 6

Ways of Knowing 3: Emotion

What is Emotion?

Like the meaning of many words the meaning of *emotion* can bewitch our intelligences.

Dictionary definitions are often more misleading than useful but the fourth definition in the New Shorter Oxford English Dictionary is helpful for our purposes.

4. Any of the natural instinctive affections of the mind (e.g. love, horror, pity) which come and go according to one's personality, experiences, and bodily state; a mental feeling.

Also mental feeling as distinguished from knowledge, and from will.

Psychologists claim to have identified over 400 distinct emotions and have divided them up into eight main 'families'.

Anger: indignation, acrimony, exasperation...

Sadness: grief, dejection, gloom...

Fear: consternation, edginess, dread...

Enjoyment: joy, pride, ecstasy...

Love: friendliness, trust, kindness...

Surprise: astonishment, amazement...

Disgust: scorn, distaste, revulsion...

Shame: guilt, remorse, contrition...

Paul Eckman, an American psychologist, claims that facial expressions indicating four of these (fear, sadness, anger and enjoyment) can be recognised by people of all cultures, from Primitive Stone Age societies to sophisticated 21st Century city dwellers

Traditionally, some philosophers regard emotion to have dubious validity as a *Ways of Knowing*. It lacks the intellectual rigour of reason and the experience of sense perception. Emotion is regarded as a personal, subjective often-indefinable *Ways of Knowing* that Plato would certainly not accept as 'knowledge' but would classify as 'belief'. Knowledge through emotion is knowledge we have through our everyday experiences and our self-awareness, instincts and intuition, and through our environment, upbringing and values. Emotion enables us to respond to music, painting, sculpture and literature and to relate to findings in the human sciences and history and of course to accepting and/or rejecting ethical ideas and arguments.

Emotion is a less rational, more personal ways-of-knowing than reason or sense perception but that does not mean it is less important. To understand emotion as a *Ways of Knowing* you have to accept it is a significant factor in our acquisition and understanding of knowledge. If you are a hard line rationalist you may find this difficult.

Reason and sense perception are never completely free of emotion and emotion as a *Ways of Knowing* is not free from reason. Helping you to appreciate the strength of emotion and its value as a *Ways of Knowing* enables you to make effective comparisons between *Ways of Knowing* and *Areas of Knowledge*, a major objective of the TOK programme.

Four 'emotion' *Ways of Knowing* are discussed in this chapter: empathy, conscience, introspection and acquaintance. Each of these four ways can be described separately but in practice, in dealing with our own emotions, they blend together. One of the issues you should address is what, for you, are the most relevant 'emotions' *Ways of Knowing* used in constructing knowledge in each of the *Areas of Knowledge*.

Emotion as a Way of Knowing: Empathy

When Anna's friend Lucy passed her driving test Anna knew how she felt. She knew this by empathy. She was able to empathise with Lucy, to understand her thoughts and feelings, and her sense of achievement.

Empathy has been much discussed and analysed by psychologists. Here are some of the features that they have defined.

Empathy is created and controlled in the brain by what are called *mirror neurons*. Mirror neurons are the brain cells that encourage people to copy other people's actions. Babies, for instance, imitate those around them and learn the emotional responses that create bonding. Mirror neurons become active when someone is watching another person experience an emotion. They encourage the observer to feel the emotions, the sense of failure, disappointment, embarrassment, and joy of the person they are observing. This also happens when reading about a character in a novel, or hearing of triumphs or disasters in the media.

Empathy involves a leap of imagination into someone else's head.

Empathy is the ability of a person to spontaneously and naturally understand another person's thoughts and feelings. Strongly empathetic people don't just understand a small number of fairly obvious thoughts and feelings, like pain and sadness; they can understand a wide range of emotional conditions.

Empathetic people respond to other people's tone of voice, scan their faces (especially the eyes) and the body postures to understand how they are feeling and what they are thinking.

Empathy makes real communication possible. It leads you to understand the person you are talking to, checking to see if they want to enter the dialogue and what they think about the subject.

Empathy also motivates the empathetic person to find out and care about other people.

Empathy is used to build moral codes. We build moral codes from our feeling for others, as well as ourselves. And part of that feeling is compassion that is generated by empathy.

Empathy enables us to understand other people's thoughts and feelings. It allows us to see the other side of an argument, another point of view, and another world picture. Empathy, it could be argued, is to the artist—the painter, the dancer, the poet, the novelist, the playwright – what empiricism is to the natural scientist: the basic tool with which he or she goes about his or her business. How could the Greeks have written the great tragedies if they had not been empathetic? How could Shakespeare have written about jealousy and ambition and the problems of ageing if he had not been able to project himself into the minds of his protagonists? How could Picasso have painted *Guernica* if he had not understood the effect of war on people's thoughts and feelings?

And for you, if you study literature or history or any of the human sciences, empathy must be at the core of your way of knowing. The very first examination assessment criterion for the Language A1 Commentary paper is

- *How well has the candidate understood the thoughts and feelings expressed in the text?*

Those 'thoughts and feelings' are the thoughts and feelings of a creative artist responding to a human situation, exploring through language an idea or an understanding. Your task, reading literature, is to respond to those thoughts and feelings. Without empathy you would not be able to do that.

Emotion as a Way of Knowing:

Conscience

We know it is wrong to steal. Our conscience tells us it is wrong. Our conscience is our sense of right and wrong; it directs our ability to judge what we should do about moral issues. It tells us, amongst other things, it is wrong

to spread malicious gossip. It tells us it is wrong to copy TOK essays from the Internet and pass them off as our own and it tells us it is wrong to 'borrow' from our baby sister's money box.

Conscience has been described as a human 'faculty', in this case a special part of the mind that is responsible for moral decisions. Everyone, it is claimed, is endowed with this faculty, but, of course, not everyone is endowed to the same extent, which explains why moral behaviour varies from person to person.

Most of us do seem to have a conscience. Where does it come from and how do we know what it tells us to do? The values our conscience applies to make moral decisions almost certainly come from the emotional and moral environment in which we were nurtured. We examine our conscience when we make moral decisions and our conscience must be a collection of those values that we have acquired in our lifetime.

The Divine Voice

Conscience has also been described as 'a reflection of the voice of God' and as such, it is claimed, 'has authority over all other sources of motivation'. Socrates claimed he had 'a divine voice' inside him, which we would certainly call his conscience. His 'divine voice' made him protest against capital punishment and it was his 'divine voice', which made him critical of the citizens of Athens and eventually led to his own death.

Emotion as a Way of Knowing:

Introspection

Kenji is nervous and a little frightened at the thought of the upcoming IB Diploma exams. He knows he is nervous and frightened by introspection. Introspection is the examination of one's own mental and emotional processes. You are aware of what you feel, hope, think, and believe. By examining your own mind you make yourself aware of what is there. These thoughts and feelings may be created and shaped by external contact, but once you have them they are independent of things outside of you. Kenji's nervousness and fear are emotions based on the feelings he has for an external object, the object in this case being the upcoming exams.

There are problems, of course, with introspection. The main one seems to be that access to our own minds, which is what introspection is, gives us access to something that can be misleading. We have all seen people in love who don't realise they are in love or who try to repress the idea that they are in love, people who will not face up to the reality of what is in their minds. Haven't you ever taken pains to ensure that you did not accept some aspect of your thinking, or feeling, that you did not wish to acknowledge? Sigmund Freud warned us that we were not the best judges of our own state of consciousness.

Another problem with introspection is that it is often difficult to describe the mental state which introspection presents. 'Oh give me a break', is what we might mutter when we feel depressed or pressured or 'under the weather', without being able to say exactly why we need a break. It is not easy to put feelings into words.

Emotion as a Way of Knowing:

Acquaintance

Bertrand Russell, a distinguished 20th century philosopher, described what he called 'knowledge-by-acquaintance'. The knowledge-by-acquaintance, he claimed, is the knowledge a 'a dog lover has of a dog'. It is 'direct and immediate', enabling us to identify the smell of freshly baked bread and prompts us to sympathise with a crying baby. Can you describe the feeling of sand under your feet? Or the smell of a dog kennel? Or how you can recognise your friends when you see them in the local shopping mall? These things you know by acquaintance.

Anna knows the moods of her friend Lucy because she is acquainted with them. She and Lucy have been friends for several years and without thinking too much about them,

Anna has grown familiar with her friend's moods: sometimes Lucy is playful, sometimes cynical, sometimes happy, sometimes a little sad. Anna knows they are part of Lucy's personality, her being. Anna would find it difficult, if not impossible, to explain how she recognises Lucy's moods, but she has no doubt that she can recognise them. Anna has knowledge of Lucy's moods by acquaintance.

Faith, Belief, Experience and Intuition.

One way of knowing, faith, which you may have expected to be considered in this chapter on emotion as a *Ways of Knowing,* is not mentioned here. Because of its importance as a way of knowing to many people, and because of the controversies that faith can, and does, cause, faith is discussed in Chapter 8 Beyond the Diagram: Faith

You may find the discussion of the TOK Linking Concepts, Belief, Experience, Intuition and Values (Chapter 15) helpful in developing your awareness of emotion as a *Ways of Knowing.*

Chapter 7

Ways of Knowing 4: Language

…all human activity seems bewitched by language. Language casts spells on all our communication, it bewitches with its connotations, flux, grammatical structures, origins, vagueness, contexts, implications, imperfections, irregularities, limited and unlimited vocabulary and because it is an enigmatic, imperfect human enterprise.

Wittgenstein

Despite its bewitching powers, language is an important *Ways of Knowing*. Knowledge is both constructed and made public by, and with, language. The IB Diploma curriculum designers were themselves bewitched by language. They have it in the middle circle of the TOK diagram as a *Ways of Knowing*. Where they do not have it is in the outer ring of the TOK diagram as an *Area of Knowledge*. One expects it to be in the outer circle, along with maths, natural science, history and the arts, as a school subject. But it isn't there. They have it twice in the Diploma hexagon, as language A1 (group 1) and as a second language (group 2). There it is, taking up a third of the diploma time, and yet it isn't classified as an *Area of Knowledge*. Bewitching.

In the context of TOK, 'language' is a *Ways of Knowing*. There are three basic questions to ask about Language as a TOK *Ways of Knowing*.

- **What is the role of language in creating knowledge?**
  How do each of the six *Areas of Knowledge* use language in creating new knowledge?Can, for instance, the natural scientists put accurately into language the ideas and relationships of the physical phenomena? Do they need language to develop their new knowledge?

- **To what extent does knowledge depend on language?**
  When historians make historical claims are they restricted in the claim by the language they use or is it only through language that the claims become possible? When poets share their thoughts and feelings about a personal perception is that sharing inevitably distorted by the language used?

- **How does language affect thinking and creativity and imagination?**
  Can there be any thinking without language? Do we think in language? Does language shape thought?

As a TOK student you need to look at how language as a *Ways of Knowing* relates to the six *Areas of Knowledge*. How important is language in creating new knowledge in Maths? In Natural and human sciences? History? Ethics? The Arts?

Much of what you have read about *Ways of Knowing* has the 'Knower(s)' at the centre of the diagram defined as those scholars and artists who create new knowledge. Change this definition to you, the students as the Knower(s) at the centre. Ask yourself how you use language to create knowledge new to you. Think of a mathematical topic you have recently studied in your classes: graphs of functions perhaps, and analyse how you came to understand graphs of functions. What part did language play in developing your understanding? Was there a point perhaps when language even got in the way of your understanding? Try the same exercise with responding to a poem. Can you recall a time when your understanding and appreciation of a poem was confused by the language?

Use the three questions above to start your analysis. What role did language play in creating your understanding of graphs of functions (or whatever other mathematical topic you have recently learned.)? To what extent did your new understanding actually depend on language? And how did language affect your own internalisation of the topic? Do you see your understanding as a series of graphs or as language describing these graphs?

Perhaps it may help to understand Language as a Way of Knowing if you understand a little about language itself.

What is Language?

We all know what 'language' is, and yet we have difficulty in defining the word 'language'. When challenged we probably consult a dictionary and there we find an approximate definition, using more language. *The New Shorter Oxford English Dictionary* (NSOED) has bewitchingly five major definitions of the word 'language', divided into fifteen minor divisions. How do you know which one to select for your definition? You have to select the definition that is most appropriate for the context in which you are being asked to define the word.

Linguistics

Linguists study linguistics, a field of scientific research with language analysis as its focus.

Universities began teaching linguistics in the 1960s. Studies are divided into three main sections.

• Theoretical linguistics constructs general principles for the study of all languages.

•   Descriptive linguistics defines the facts of a particular language system and

• Comparative linguistics examines the similarities and differences between languages.

At one point early in the planning of the IB Diploma it was considered that Linguistics be a compulsory subject. The planners believed that linguistics would teach a general awareness of the nature of language, which they described as 'a great tool of thought'. Linguistics was rejected in favour of a second language.

Language Functions

One of the concerns of linguists is attempting to understand the nature of language by the functions it performs. There are almost as many classifications of the functions of language as there are books about it.

> Wittgenstein gave one of the most comprehensive lists of the functions of language.
>
> *Language* he writes, *can be used to give orders; describe the appearance of an object or give its measurement; report an event; speculate about an event; form and test a hypothesis; present the results of an experiment; make up a story; play act; sing catches; guess riddles; make a joke and tell it; solve a problem in practical arithmetic; translate from one language to another; ask, think, greet, cure and pray.*

Despite the many classifications of the functions of language most linguists agree on the significant features of language.

Language, they say

- is uniquely human

- communicates

- uses symbols.

  The NSOED definition closest to this consensus definition is 'a system of human communication using words, written and spoken, and particular ways of combining them'.

Whether language is uniquely human or not is an interesting discussion, but is not really a TOK issue. But, language as communication, and the way language uses symbols, certainly is.

Language Communicates

Linguists classify communication through language into three groups: transactional communication, expressive communication and internal communication.

Transactional communication.

The most obvious function of language (i.e. of the messages it communicates) is that it is transactional. Transactional here means 'to get things done'. In this category it is used, amongst other things to:

- give information (Sun Yat-sen was proclaimed President of the Republic of China in 1912);

- give instructions (Stop when the light is red);

- set up a hypothesis (If these plants do not receive water they will die);

- solve problems (Add the lengths of the sides of the field together and you calculate the amount of fencing you need).

In these examples of the transactional use of language, the meaning of the language in the message, if the message is to communicate clearly, must be unambiguous. Inevitably when abstract ideas are part of the message, different understandings of the meaning of words and the way they are presented can interfere seriously with the communication, both with others and oneself.

Expressive communication

Language can also be used to communicate expressively, to express the feelings of the sender and to affect, not just inform, the receiver. In this kind of communication we pay special attention to the words themselves and the feelings and atmosphere they create. We find this kind of language used in poetry. Language used to communicate expressively the feelings of the sender of the message and to affect the listener, is often connotative. Connotative means imply more meaning to a word than its primary meaning. Obviously when meaning is implied the message is going to be open to interpretation, each receiver interpreting it slightly differently according to his or her own connotation.

Internal communication: Language as communication with oneself

When you sit at home in the evening and settle down to your homework do you organise the thoughts in your head using language? Do you say to yourself, in your mind 'First I'll do the math and then, if I have time I'll do the French, but before I do anything I'll just call Anna and see what she's doing'? Do you ever actually say your thoughts out loud or find yourself moving your lips as if you were speaking but not making the sounds? Do your thoughts, your communication with yourself, need to be put into language?

Some 'thinking' obviously doesn't need to be put into words. Visual artists and composers can 'see' and 'hear' what they eventually produce, without using words, and our response to the smell of freshly baked bread or the sight of a mangled car after a crash is independent of words, although the extent to which these last two examples are 'thinking' in any sense at all is questionable. If we can't put thoughts into words we can't be sure what it is we are thinking. This idea was summarised by Russian linguist Vigotsky who was quite clear in his opinion. 'Thought is born through words ... a thought unembodied [1] remains a shadow. We seem to need to put our thoughts into some sort of linguistic order and language seems to enables us to do that.'

The relationship between language and thought is a matter of speculation. There are two conflicting theories about the relationship. The first theory claims that thought and language are entirely separate, but dependent. This can mean that either language is dependent on thought or thought on language. The second theory claims that language and thought are absolutely meshed together: thinking without language is impossible. The most well known discussion of the language—thought relationship is The Sapir-Whorf Hypothesis that suggests that our thoughts are controlled by our language. Recently some psycholinguists have contested the Sapir-Whorf Hypothesis, arguing that thought and language are independent.

For the purpose of understanding ourselves as knowers it is not necessary to take sides although it is certainly worth spending a little time thinking (using language?) about the controversy. What is clear is that language is part of our thinking process. We use language to express our thoughts, to communicate and clarify our thoughts to ourselves and to others.

Language uses symbols

Humans can make certain things stand for other things. In math you are familiar with this idea. In the statement

Let h stand for the length of the hypotenuse

'h' is a symbol for a finite number representing the length of all the hypotenuses you can imagine.

---

1   'unembodied' here is interestingly bewitching: it means ' not put into words'.

In English grammar you have probably found the formula for a simple sentence,
S>V>O,

in which the symbol

> S stands for the subject,
> V for the verb and
> O for the object.

We can, by agreement, make symbols stand for anything we wish.

As part of our evolutionary development we have agreed that when we make certain sounds, when we use language, those sounds, language, are symbols. Those of us who speak English have agreed on one set of sounds as symbols and those of us who speak Chinese have agreed on another set of sounds as symbols. The sounds are agreed symbols within our language communities. A member of the English speaking community might make a sound which we write as 'Look! A small green snake'2. Any members of the community who heard the sound could, if they so chose, look and see an object that they would recognise as a small green snake. The sounds small and green and snake are symbols that are meaningful to members of that speaking community and they would know what to expect when they looked. But there is not necessarily a connection between the sound symbol and the thing or idea or stands for. The sound symbol for snake is not the reality of the snake.

This may seem a fairly obvious statement to make and with the example of the snake of course it is. But at a more abstract level the difference between the symbol and idea or thing the symbol represents is not always apparent. The word or sound can become confused with reality and the spell of language can begin to bewitch. The words green and small are beginning this process. What does 'green' symbolise? You describe your new pet snake to me as 'green' and I have an approximate idea of its

2 Writing is of course a set of symbols itself, symbols representing sound. Writing therefore is a symbol of a symbol.

colour, based on my experience of green snakes I have seen, but your snake might be a bright lime green and the snakes I have seen may be dark bottle green. I might have entirely the wrong idea of the colour of your snake. And what about small? Now the last snake you had, which escaped into the local sewage system last week may have been a six metre long anaconda, and this one, a baby anaconda to replace the monster that escaped may be only one metre long. Sure, your new snake is small compared to the one that got away, but to me a metre long snake is huge. The words, the symbols, we are using to communicate mean different things to different people in different contexts. The sender of the symbol may be clear what message he or she is sending. The receiver may be clear what message he or she is receiving. But the received signal is fundamentally different from the sent signal. The words have bewitched our intelligences: we have begun to interpret the symbols as representing reality, but there is no reality. What is green? What is small? As our acquaintance with words—symbols of reality but not reality—grows more abstract and those ideas the words symbolise become more abstract, the more we are likely to be bewitched. Because a word exists we expect it to correspond to the reality we know. Scientists have pointed out this danger as they seek to name newly discovered phenomena with old words. Black Holes are neither black nor holes but for most of us these words cast a spell. We apply the everyday meaning of the words and struggle to understand how anything black and shaped like a hole (and what shape is a hole?) can be floating around there in outer space. We are bewitched into conceptualising a reality that doesn't exist.

It is not the individual words alone that bewitch. The pattern of the language, the way the symbols are joined together, can also cast a spell. 'This path leads to the banana plantation' is a realistic straightforward statement that symbolises reality. 'This path leads to damnation' is a similar structure but the ideas implicit in it are quite different. The path of the second sentence is as different from the path of the first sentence as a banana plantation is different from damnation but the structure of the sentences can bewitch us into thinking they are quite similar: a path is a path is a path and a banana plantation is damnation. Beware the snake wrapped round the banana tree tempting you with the fruit of knowledge.

Further Bewitchment

That language communicates and uses symbols and that it both communicates and uses symbols in a variety of ways is clear. What isn't always clear is how well language communicates and uses symbols. This chapter begins with a quotation from Wittgenstein: *'Philosophy is a battle against the bewitchment of our intelligence by means of language.'* It is worth staying with this idea of bewitchment. Language bewitches us all and the first bewitchment we should look at is implied in our original definition. Language, as defined by linguists is uniquely human, communicates and uses symbols. We have looked briefly at language as communication and seen how it can bewitch with its use of symbols. Here are more ways in which language bewitches us.

The Meaning of Words

It is a generally held belief that words have a true meaning and to be able to use a word accurately we must be aware of that true meaning. To appreciate this meaning we are advised to look at words, see how they are used, and then come to an awareness of the true meaning. What often happens is a word can mean so many things in so many situations we simply can't do this. Many words have no true meaning; rather they have so many different meanings that can only be appreciated in context. The potential power of such words to bewitch is immense: how can your intelligence function clearly if the words you use to think and to express your thoughts can mean many different things? Dictionary makers know this. They obtain their definitions from the way words are used. The full title of the *Shorter Oxford English Dictionary* is *The New Shorter Oxford Dictionary on Historical Principles*. The historical principles are important. The editors of the dictionary read widely and they noted every interesting or unusual word and unfamiliar uses of common words within the context of the sentences they read. When the word is defined for the dictionary the editors look at all the uses of the word they have compiled, and the dates these usages were current, and come to their definition based on the meaning of the words in the context, both now and in the past. The changes in the meaning of a word are traced historically. In time the meaning of words shift and change for many reasons and we can only be sure of the meaning when we know its time context as well as its context within a sentence. Several hundred years ago the word *lust* meant *innocent delight*. The entry for *gay* in the NOED has thirteen definitions, the first dating back to Middle English, (the language spoken in England between 1150 and 1349)[3]. Only the last entry, from the mid-20th century, has anything to do with the meaning homosexual.

---

3   Old English is not the language used by Shakespeare. He used the Elizabethan form of modern English. Old English is the form of English spoken in England up to the middle of the 12th century. *Old* here has a technical meaning within the history of language. Another example of the bewitching meaning of words.

If *cockroaches* were called *cuddle-bugs*, would they seem nicer? If Hitler had used the original family name of *Schicklgruber* would he have done quite so much damage? According to Marshall Blonsky, a Wolfson Fellow in semiotics at the New School of New York, USA, "The sound of a word is of enormous importance. The sound is the lubricant that gets the signifier and its meaning into our consciousness". "If you've got a lot of names for something," Blonsky says, "none of them euphonious, then it's as if you don't have any name. And if you don't have a name for a thing, then as far as most people are concerned, you don't have the thing at all."

When her teacher says Anna is a 'good' student she means 'diligent' but when the same teacher says Anna gets 'good' grades she means 'high'. When her mother says Anna is a 'good' daughter she might mean 'keeps out of trouble'. When Anna's friend says Anna is a 'good' friend she means 'faithful', when her grandfather says she has a 'good' deal of common sense he uses the word differently from when he says she is a 'good' girl. We must look at the context of each statement to understand the meaning of 'good'. A multitude of words have meaning only in context. When we isolate them to define them they become meaningless. Even in context they still bewitch. What could Anna's mother mean when she says Anna is a 'good' girl? It might just mean she doesn't smoke or that she brings her a cup of coffee every morning or it might mean Anna is a model of conventional morality.

Sometimes the meaning of words is so vague it is difficult to understand their meaning at all. We have already seen *small* and *green*. Giving instructions to someone is fraught with difficulties. What does 'Turn right just as you enter the village' mean? Does it mean turn sharply right or fork to the right? And 'just' means what? 'As soon as'? 'Immediately'? And does 'village' mean where the village boundary is signposted or where the houses begin?

Words that have almost the same meaning can also bewitch. *Hint, intimate, insinuate, suggest,* and *imply* can be very similar in meaning and we would probably not agree on the subtle differences, if any, in the meaning of each one unless we were aware of the exact context in which it is being used. Poets, of course, delight in the uncertainty of the meaning of words and weave them together in fascinating patterns to further reinforce their ambiguity. Here is the start of a poem by Gerard Manley Hopkins, a poem that bewitches with its choice of words and images.

Glory be to God for dappled things -

For skies of couple-colour as a brinded cow;

For rose-moles all in stipple upon trout that swim;

Fresh-firecoal chestnut-falls; finches' wings;

Landscape plotted and pieced - fold, fallow and plough;

And all trades, their gear and tackle and trim.

You will not find *rose-moles* or *chestnut-falls* in a dictionary. All this bewitchment about the meaning of words doesn't mean dictionaries are of no use and we should throw them away. Dictionaries can indicate the possible meaning of words, a meaning the reader has to take and put in context. Beware of them, though. Dictionaries cast their own spell: you think you have the meaning, after all it is written there in the dictionary, and what you have is only a possible meaning.

Language Creates Reality

In the 1990s it became fashionable to mock 'politically correct' (PC) language. The classification 'politically correct' is itself an example of words bewitching. 'Socially correct' might be more appropriate, but that could be interpreted as a guide to good manners. In some ways that is what PC language is, an attempt to prune offensive, sexist, prejudiced, racist terms from the language because they create offence. But they also create reality. Recently I re-read Mark Twain's Huckleberry Finn, and as I was finishing it I visited New York and stayed with an old friend who had just retired. His wife still goes off to work everyday and at breakfast on the first day of my visit I asked him, as he sliced the bagels and perked the coffee, what it was like being the house nigger. (Remember I was reading *Huckleberry Finn)*. My friend stopped cutting his bagel; paused, and said very seriously to me, 'Don't use that word'. And such was the intensity of his command I have not used it since. The word is unacceptable, and for good reason. It was offensive to the people it described and it reflected a social and economic status that no longer exists. And one of the reasons that status no longer exists is because the word is no longer used. The language that reflected reality also created and maintained it. The feminists are right, if we always read of doctors as 'he' and nurses as 'she', we eventually begin to expect reality to reflect that situation. The words create the reality and our intelligences are bewitched.

Language Infers and Judges

An inference is a conclusion you come to about the unknown based on something you know. 'Anna is clever', you might infer, from the facts you know. She always gets good grades and hands her work in promptly without any obvious effort. But your statement is not a fact but an inference. Anna may work very hard, she may struggle over every piece of written work she hands in and she may spend hours discussing her work with her parents or her brother. What you are saying when you say she is clever is simply that she gets good grades and hands her work in on time. Your inference that she is clever achieves a status it does not deserve. The words have bewitched you into believing something that is open to question is, in fact, a reality.

What you have done is made a judgment and the words of your judgement may imply a disapproval or approval that is not necessarily valid. The bewitchment is that judgements, once they have been put into words, obstruct thought. What does 'Anna is a wonderful human being' actually mean? The person who made the statement probably means that Anna's values, and the way she presents her values, are the same as their own In extreme cases the judgement is obvious. If someone is called a 'scumbag' or the 'sweetest person on earth' it is clear a judgement is being made. But often phrases and words are used which are just as judgmental but not obviously so. 'He was a typical Wall Street money trader', implies all sorts of judgements and stereotypes. The stereotyping bewitches the intelligence. This is a generalised judgement.

Language Classifies

'You know the problem with the cafeteria at lunchtime. It's those eighth graders. There are so many of them. They are so noisy and they jump the line. They are awful.'

When you describe the eighth graders in this way you classify them. The individuals belong to no class until we, with our language, put them in it. And in this case our classification will probably lead us to believe the worst of the eighth graders whenever we meet them. If one of them is noisy on the school bus—that's typical. If one of them doesn't work—that's typical. If one of them doesn't turn up for a basketball match—that's typical.

Classifying, frequently determines our attitudes and behaviour towards those things that are classified. Eighth graders are no different from ninth, tenth, eleventh and twelfth graders. They have just the same mix of lazy and hardworking, noisy and quiet, extrovert and introvert individuals as any other grade, but once they are classified in our minds as a particular set of abstractions the language of the classifications bewitches.

Jews, Arabs, socialists, communists, hippies, drop outs, saints, valley girls, republicans, these are all generalisations. Do any of these words really mean anything or are they just a set of sounds that trigger in us conventional reactions?

Language is Always Changing

Language is always changing; you know this from your personal experience, as I do. I often sit open mouthed in astonishment and awe at some of the vibrant language I hear used by Diploma students. I am well impressed.

Change in usage brings vibrancy and vigour to a language, but is often resisted by more conservative (or insecure?) members of the community. Each of the dialects of English— American, Canadian, Irish, Caribbean, Australian, etc. etc., has changed and still changes, and enrich the language. Slang and unconventional usage also brings dynamism to communication that standard usage doesn't.

*****

I have only begun here to explore how language bewitches our intelligences, our Ways of Knowing and the ideas and concepts in those disciplines we study. Language is what the linguists define it as: it is uniquely human, it does communicate and it uses symbols. But it also bewitches your intelligence and casts spells on reason, emotion and sense perception. Use it as a Ways of Knowing with great caution.

Chapter 8

Areas of Knowledge
Beyond the Diagram:
Faith as a Way of Knowing

TOK is a subject created for the IB Diploma and the four *Ways of Knowing* are an attempt to present a simplified version of the many complex ways in which we are able to know. Inevitably there are omissions. Perhaps the most significant Way of Knowing that is not in the TOK diagram is faith.

Faith is only briefly mentioned in the Curriculum Guide and clearly the writers of the guide consider it as part of emotion. In the Emotion section, under Nature of Emotion (page 20) the question is asked, *Is faith an emotion, a feeling, or neither?* And on the same page under Linking Questions (Emotion) are the two merged questions, *Is faith purely emotional or is it possible to provide a rational justification for religious belief? Is emotion a source of spiritual knowledge?*

Faith also makes only an occasional appearance in the prescribed essay list. It appears in May 2012 where students are invited to respond to the question, *Analyse the strengths and weaknesses of using faith as a basis for knowledge in religion and in one other area of knowledge from the TOK diagram?* (The question seems to imply that religion is an *Area of Knowledge* in the TOK diagram.)

Faith is certainly a powerful force in the 21st century and it is likely that for many IB Diploma students faith is a major *Way of Knowing*. For these two reasons I include this brief comment.

Humans started to worship God (or gods), to have faith, as soon as they learned to stand upright. This faith arose from their wonder and awe of the natural world they inhabited and an attempt to find meaning and value in their lives, and their place in that world. And, to help them find this meaning and value, they created gods. Gods, and their faith in them, is probably the most powerful force in the history of the human race.

In the Palaeolithic period, when agriculture was developing, the cult of the Mother Goddess expressed a sense that the fertility that was transforming human life was sacred. Artists carved statues showing her naked and pregnant and these statues have been found all over Europe, the Middle East and India. The Mother Goddess remained important for centuries. She was called Inana in Sumeria, Ishtar in Babylon, Anat in Canaan, Isis in Egypt and Aphrodite in Greece. In each of these cultures she was worshipped and stories about her abounded. The stories were not taken literally but helped people to be aware of the sense of what they perceived as the unseen forces surrounding them and controlling their lives.

These 'unseen forces' are at the heart of faith. People wanted to get in touch with these forces, to work with them and to admire them. When we personalise these unseen forces and make them gods we are expressing our sense of affinity with them and the world in which they live.

Throughout history we have experienced this dimension of life that goes beyond our everyday, pragmatic existence. However we choose to interpret this transcendence, as it has been often called, it is a fact of our historical development. Many societies have called this transcendence God and have been awed by the concept they have created. Jews are not allowed to pronounce the sacred name of God; Moslems must not depict the divine visually. Despite the rejection of the idea of God by modern, western secular society, a recent survey shows that 80% of Americans believe that God created the universe. Both in the past and in the present, faith is a very potent way of knowing.

An example of faith: Newman and 'conscience'

One of the great western explorers of the nature of faith was the 19th century cardinal, John Henry Newman. The foundation of Newman's approach to faith lies in the concept of conscience. His deep respect for conscience is perhaps best seen in a short passage from his novel *Callista*, published in 1855. *Callista* describes the conversion to Christianity of a North African sculptor and her eventual martyrdom. She describes her burgeoning awareness of conscience in conversation to a non-Christian philosopher:

I feel that God within my heart. I feel myself in His presence. He say to me, 'Do this, don't do that'. You may tell me that this dictate is a mere law of my nature, as to joy or to grieve. I cannot understand this. No it is the echo of a person speaking to me. Nothing shall persuade me that it does not ultimately proceed from a person external to me. It carries with it its proof of its divine origin. My nature feels towards it as towards a person....I believe in what is more than a mere 'something'. I believe in what is more real to me than sun, moon, stars, and the fair earth, and the voice of friends. You will say, Who is He? Has He ever told you anything about Himself? Alas! No! - more's the pity. But I will not give up what I have, because I have not more. An echo implies a voice; a voice a speaker. That speaker I love and fear.

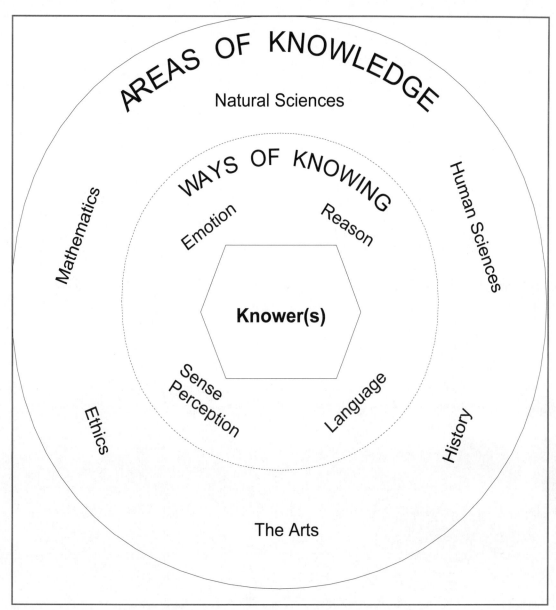

AREAS OF KNOWLEDGE

Natural Sciences

WAYS OF KNOWING

Human Sciences

Mathematics

Emotion

Reason

Knower(s)

Sense Perception

Language

Ethics

History

The Arts

ToK Diagram

In your TOK classes you will critically examine how knowledge is constructed or created in the six *Areas of Knowledge* in the outer circle of the TOK diagram. Each of these Areas has been chosen because of its uniqueness as an *Area of Knowledge*.

Mathematicians, historians, ethicists, artists and, natural and human scientists all search for, and construct, knowledge in different ways.

When you understand the different ways knowledge is constrcted then you can begin to evaluate that knowledge in the context in which it is offered.

Chapter 9

Areas of Knowledge 1: Natural Sciences.

Natural Science as an area of knowledge became an obsession in the 20th century. Natural science, we have come to believe, is reliable, precise, objective, testable and self-correcting. It has, at its core, the unremitting vigilance of scientists examining evidence they collect about the nature of the natural world and ruthlessly applying logic to any analysis of that evidence. We assume the facts science gives us are true and justified. Science uses 'the scientific method'. Other disciplines model their claims to know on 'the scientific method'.

Much has been written by scientists, historians of science and philosophers about the nature of scientific knowledge. The 'scientific method', the process by which scientific knowledge is acquired, has been scrutinised so intensively that every attempt to define it has led to definitions, counter-definitions, redefinitions and reservations.

There is, however, a generally accepted popular understanding of the scientific method. For convenience let us call this the Basic Scientific Method, although the formal name *is naive inductivism*.

The Basic Scientific Method

Scientists observe the world through their senses and record the information their senses provide. They collect as much of this sensory information as they can, from as many observations as possible. Using this information they make generalisations about the things they have observed. These generalisations form the basis of a theory that explains why the information they have collected is as it is. The theory will also predict what is likely to happen in similar circumstances in the future.

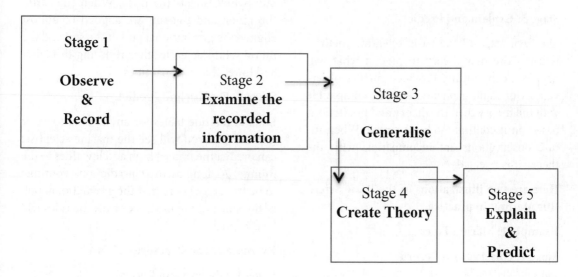

Stage 1: Observe and Record

Using their sense perception, and instruments which heighten their sense perception, natural scientists observe the phenomena of the natural world (carefully avoiding unpredictable human behaviour) keeping careful records of their observations. These observations may be direct observations of natural events, or observations of planned experiments.

Stage 2: Examine the recorded information

They then critically examine the information they have received, checking for any contradictions or inconsistencies and making further observations if needed.

Stage 3: Generalise

When they are as certain as they can be that the information they have is accurate, they examine it looking for patterns, forms and consistencies that can lead to generalisations about the phenomena they are observing.

Stage 4: Create Theory

From these generalisations they create new scientific theories about the nature of the phenomena they have been observing. These theories are always provisional, only valid until they are proved invalid.

Stage 5: Explain and Predict

The final stage of the basic scientific method is using the new theory to predict what will happen in the future. Provided further observations of natural phenomena are compatible with the theory then the theory and predictions based on it continue to be accepted. When future observations are incompatible with the theory it is rejected.

Here are two illustrations of the Basic Scientific Method in practice.

Example 1: Marine Tides

Stage 1: Observe and Record.

Marine scientists observe the rise and fall of marine tides around the world, recording the information. To make accurate measurements tide gauges at precise, fixed locations measure the water level over time. Records of both water level and time are kept.

Stage 2: Examine the information.

They examine and collate the information from the gauges checking the data is correct and looking for patterns and relationships within the data. They noticed the times and size of the tides are connected in some way with the alignment of the sun and the moon and by the pattern of ocean currents and the shape of the coastline.

Stage 3: Generalise

Using the information they make generalisations about tides throughout the world.

Stage 4: Create Theory

Using these generalisations they create a theory that the gravitational effect of the sun and the moon controlled the tides. At its simplest the theory is that the moon orbits the earth in the same direction as the earth rotates on its axis, so it takes slightly more than a day, about fifty minutes more, for the moon to return to the same place in the sky and therefore the tides rise and fall in a pattern slightly more than twelve hours. The sun also exerts a gravitational pull, which affects the tides. When the earth, the moon and the sun are aligned or almost aligned the gravitational pull of the sun and the moon reinforce each other resulting in higher and lower than normal tides.

Stage 5: Explain and Predict

Look at the tide tables for any coastal town or harbour and you will see the marine scientists can predict the time of high and low tides to the minute. As long as their predictions continue to be true, the theory that the gravitational pull of the sun and the moon controls the tides will be accepted.

Example 2: The structure of DNA

Stage 1: Observe and Record

Before Watson and Crick made public their theory of the molecular structure of DNA many other scientists searched for understanding of the molecule that carries genetic information from one generation to another. In the middle of the 19th century The Czech monk Mendel had experimented with peas and he was able to show that certain physical characteristics in peas, for instance, shape and colour were inherited in what we now call genes. A few year later a Swiss doctor, Friedrich Miescher, isolated a compound from the nuclei of cells. He called this compound nucleic acid, what we now know as the NA in DNA. It wasn't until 1944 that an American scientist, Oswald Avery, proved genes were constructed with nucleic acid. Avery's work was well publicised among the scientific community and it became widely accepted that nucleic acid held the secret that controlled the hereditary material in humans and all other living organisms. They also knew, through the work of Erwin Chargoff that the nucleic acid molecule contains equal amounts of adenine and thymine (30%) and guanine and cytosine.(20%). In short, much observing and recording had been taking place over a long period of time.

Stage 2: Examine the information

So by 1951 there was a lot of information available about the possible structure of the 'life' molecule. Rosalind Franklin, a scientist at King's College in London was attempting to determine the shape of this nucleic acid molecule using an experimental approach with x-ray images. In Cambridge Watson and Crick tried to make sense of the information by making physical models.

Stage 3: Generalise

It was one of Franklyn's x-ray images that finally revealed the structure of the molecule to Watson and Crick. Studying it they noticed a fuzzy X at its centre, using both deductive and inductive reasoning they came to the conclusion the molecule must be in the shape of a double helix.

Stage 4: Create Theory

With this x-ray image and the information about adenine-guanine and cytosine thymine bonds Crick and Watson constructed a model of the molecule as double helix with the bonds of equal length making the rungs in a double helix. Once the model was constructed it became clear DNA could be the carrier of the genetic code. Because of the structure of the molecule it is able to split into two pieces. A new molecule is formed from each piece and due to the specific adenine-guanine and cytosine-thymine pairings identical molecules are produced. They constructed their theory as compatible with the information available to them.

Stage 5: Explain and Predict

Although the scientists of the 1950s were not aware of it when they made their dramatic discoveries about the structure of DNA it has powerful predictive qualities. The knowledge of how genetic material is stored and copied has given a new way to looking at biological processes. Amongst other things diseases that are caused by a lack of a particular protein can be treated by gene therapy.

Ways of Knowing in the Natural Sciences.

The TOK diagram gives us a restricted choice. As TOK students we must ask ourselves how scientists use the four Ways of Knowing, reason, language, sense perception and emotion when they create new knowledge and, of course, we must then question the reliability of these *Ways of Knowing* within the context of natural science.

Stage 1: Observe and Record

The first stage is observation, beginning with *sense perception*. Stage one begins with *sense perception*. The first stage is observation. Scientists begin to construct new knowledge using their senses, by observations of the physical phenomena of the world. To be valid, scientific observations must be accurate and unbiased. We know already how easy it is for our senses to be deceived, making our observations inaccurate and misleading. (See Perception,

Chapter Five). Our senses cannot be trusted. Of course scientists are aware of this problem and take great care with their observations.

Stage one also involves *language* as a way of knowing Observations have to be described in language. There has to be what is called an 'observation statement'. This statement will be scrutinised and used by other scientists. But even the simplest observation statement, because it uses language, can be subject to a variety of interpretations. For instance, here is an observational statement about tides, in simple everyday language: *The highest tide was recorded at 14.42.* Much is assumed in this statement. It is assumed there is such a thing as a tide, an immense concept in itself. It is also assumed it is possible to have a highest tide, which implies a lowest and a mean and the concept of height. Is the concept of height really appropriate in describing the movement of water? Isn't there an implication that the sea level is constantly changing? The precision of the observational statement is as precise as the language used and the ideas that are embedded in that language. However neutral the initial observation is, the language of the observation statement inevitably influences that neutrality.

Stage 2: Examine the recorded information

The Way of Knowing at stage two changes to *reason*. Scientists look at the information they have and search for patterns and explanations of the phenomena. They use their reasoning power to look for logical explanations of the patterns they observe. But to do this they need to use imagination and sometimes intuition, both of which could be regarded as using *emotion* as a Way of Knowing. They almost certainly use *language* to organise their thinking and their findings and to discuss them with their colleagues.

Stage 3: Generalise

Generalising uses *reason* in the form of inductive logic. You already know the problem with inductive logic, the unreliability of generalisations. Science is looking for cer-

tainty. Inductive logic does not give certainty. It can give good reasons for supporting a conclusion but it can never guarantee it. Deductively one might argue

• The scientific method demands certainty

• Inductive logic can never be certain

• Therefore the scientific method cannot use inductive logic.

This creates what is known, rather grandly, as the Problem of Induction.

We earlier attempted to use inductive logic to test the generalisation using three tests, the Sufficient Number Test, the Varying Circumstances Test and the Exceptions Test, (see Chapter 4). If the generalisation passes these three tests we can suggest probability rather than certainty.

Generalising of course involves *language* with, inevitably, the possibility of bewitchment.

Stages 4: Creating a Theory.

The creating of a theory should be pure deductive *reason*. Deductive logic, you will recall, guarantees that if the premises of an argument are sound then the argument must be valid. The problem of course is that the 'facts', the premises, have been created by inductive reason. Theories and the thought processes that create them are of course using *language*.

Stage 5: Explaining and Predicting

Again the *Ways of Knowing* here are deductive *reason* and *language*. Reason is used to claim that if the theory is valid now it should be valid in the future. Language is used to explain the claim and to communicate it.

So from a TOK diagram perspective the natural sciences start with a firm *sense perception* foundation and are carried along with inductive and deductive *reason*, with language used to create ideas and explain them. Where does this leave *emotion*?

Scientists are human. They don't just observe whatever is there to be observed they choose what they observe. They 'choose' for as many reasons as there are scientists. They choose for financial reasons (what industry will pay for); for social reasons, (what societies see as important); for political reasons, (what governments want) for practical reasons (what equipment is available); for personal reasons (to advance their career) and so on. Science is also influenced by trends: at the moment it is fashionable to concern oneself with the problems of the global warning. The observations scientists make are inevitably influenced by the reason they are observing. *Emotion* is used here to motivate the scientists, not to create new knowledge.

Despite the problems with sense perception, inductive logic and language, natural science works. It delivers. Predictions about the tides have been proved to be right so far. Laws of nature may not be certain but they probably are. The more observations we make, the more information we have confirming what we know, then the more likely it is to be true. So, the tide may not rise and fall tomorrow but it probably, very probably, will.

Alternatives to the Basic Scientific Method: Falsification and Scientific Revolution.

Some scientists and philosophers argue strongly The Basic Scientific Method is not really the basis of scientific knowledge. Two well known alternatives you may have heard of are Karl Popper's *Principle of Falsification* and Thomas Kuhn's Theory of *Scientific Revolution*.

Principle of Falsification

From the diagram on page 6 you can see that the Principle of Falsification depends as much on observation as the Basic Scientific Method. The difference, amongst other things, is that this method does not begin with observation. The observation, the empirical experiment, is undertaken after the theory has been stated and with the sole view of falsifying. Popper's method is as dependent on observation, and therefore, as subject to the problems of sense perception, as the Basic Scientific Method. What it is not subject to is the Problem of Induction. No generalisations, and therefore no inductive logic, are used. Popper's Theory has three obvious advantages over the Basic Scientific Method: certainty, scientific relevance and growth.

KARL POPPER'S PRINCIPLE OF FALSIFICATION

1. Certainty
Falsification has one clear advantage over the Basic Scientific Method. If one single false example shows the hypothesis to be unacceptable, it is unsatisfactory, it cannot be 'scientific'. Therefore a certainty is achieved: the certainty there is no certainty. With the Basic Scientific Method no matter how many observations are made which support an hypothesis, there can never be certainty. The next, as yet unmade observation, may disprove the theory.

2. Scientific Relevance
Falsification has another advantage. It can be used to distinguish scientific valid hypotheses from non-scientific hypotheses. An hypothesis that cannot be falsified cannot be scientific. *Earthquakes under the Pacific Ocean always occur in June* is an easy hypothesis to test by empirical experimentation, by observation, and to falsify or not, so it has scientific potential. *That there will, or will not, be earthquakes under the Pacific Ocean in June* is not a scientific hypothesis because it cannot be falsified. You cannot test the theory that there will, or will not be, an earthquake under the Pacific in June. The statement is true by definition.

3. Scientific Growth
Falsification encourages the growth of scientific knowledge. Science progresses when hypotheses are falsified and new, and better, theories replace them. Science progresses in this trial and error way. If you cannot, theoretically, falsify a hypothesis then it will not lead to new knowledge.

Does Popper's Principle of Falsification reflect accurately how science has progressed in the last two thousand years? Two major developments in the history of science would suggest the answer to this question might be 'No'.

For about 1500 years the Ptolemaic view of the universe put the earth at its centre. In the late 15th century Copernicus after observing the sun and the planets conceived the idea that the earth and the other planets in our solar system, moved round the sun. Despite the consider-able evidence he presented to his fellow scientists falsifying the Ptolemaic view, it was several centuries before his ideas were accepted. Sir Isaac Newton's laws of gravity and motion were accepted and applied for over two centuries. They had, in part, been falsified soon after they were published, by observations of the moon's orbit. Only in the 20th century did Albert Einstein, through falsification of parts of them, show they had to be revised or modified.

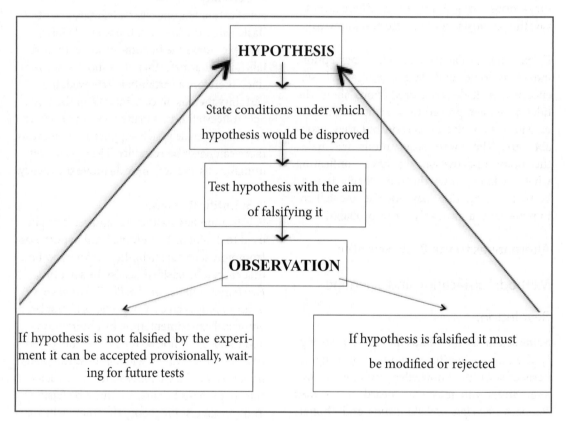

Karl Popper's Principle of Falsification

The empirical basis of objective science has thus nothing 'absolute' about it. Science does not rest upon rock bottom. The bold structure of its theories rises, as it were, above a swamp. It is like a building erected on piles...driven down from far above into the swamp, but not to any natural or given base; and when we cease our attempt to drive our piles into a deeper layer, it is not because we have reached firm ground. We simply stop when we are satisfied that they are firm enough to carry the structure, or at least for the time being.

Karl Popper

Scientific Revolution

A physicist turned scientific historian, Thomas Kuhn, argues that neither the Basic Scientific Method nor Falsification reflects what happens in reality. Kuhn argues that science progresses through 'revolutions'. A scientific revolution, like any other revolution, is a movement in which one system is replaced, dramatically, by another system. Reduced to its simplest level Kuhn's argument is this:

Within a restricted scientific community, say taxonomy within biology, the acceptance of what Kuhn calls a *paradigm* emerges. All the scientists working within this taxonomic community work within a collection of assumptions, laws and theories which they accept as rigorous and normal. Taxonomists agree on certain principles for the classification of, say, insects. As they go about their work, classifying insects, they relate their observations of insects to the paradigm that is the normal science of their particular scientific community. They adjust and modify their paradigm if falsifications become apparent but consistently stay within it. Eventually there comes a point when new observations are no longer compatible with the existing paradigm. It may be that progress in another branch of biology, say knowledge of the DNA of genes, gives them information about insects that is incompatible with the existing paradigm. Revolution. The old paradigm goes and is replaced by a new one. This new paradigm, which is based on the new assumptions, laws and theories arising from knowledge of DNA, attracts more and more taxonomists and becomes the paradigm, their new normal science. This paradigm becomes accepted until it too is overthrown.

Chapter 10

Areas of Knowledge 2: Mathematics

The Greek mathematician Euclid is famous for his great work, *Elements of Geometry*, which he wrote about 300BC. *Elements of Geometry* begins with a systematic explanation of plane (two dimensional) geometry still taught in schools today. Euclid's method of creating this mathematical knowledge is a clear example of how mathematical knowledge is created and formalised.

He started his explanations by assuming a small set of concepts, called *axioms*. These axioms are at the heart of mathematics and so it is important to understand where they come from. Euclid *assumed* them. That is he accepted them as being true, without proof, for the purpose of argument.

At the start of his section on plane geometry he listed the five assumed axioms on which his geometry was based. Here they are:

Euclid's Axioms *(Sometimes called Euclid's Postulates)*

- Two points determine a line segment.

- A line segment can be extended indefinitely along a line.

- A circle can be drawn with a centre and a radius.

- All right angles are congruent.

- If two lines are cut by another line (called a transversal) and the interior angles on the same side of the transversal have a total measure of 180° then the lines will intersect on that side of the transversal.

These assumed axioms underpin all his plane geometry. Euclid *assumed* these axioms with his intellectual insight, sometimes called 'intuitive knowledge'. It is knowledge, which is accepted - assumed - as obvious, self-evident. What mathematicians have been doing ever since is use reason, reason completely independent of sense perception, to create sets of rules defined with language. Once these rules are defined and accepted all further mathematical ideas and theorems, are construed from them using deductive reasoning

Most mathematicians are not directly concerned with axioms. They know axioms are the rock bottom foundations of mathematics but find it difficult to define them. They assume them as 'given' and work with theorems developed from them. They would probably claim that, if necessary or desirable, they could define the particular axioms on which their work is based, but they seldom have reason to do this.

There are, of course, different sets of axioms for different parts of mathematics. In 1908 Ernst Zermelo and Abraham Fraenkel defined a set of axioms known as are the Seven Axioms of Set Theory . The truth of these Zermelo-Fraenkel axioms, it has been argued, 'is established by intuitions, which lie too deep for proof since all proof depends on them'.

A well publicised set of axioms is known as the Peano Postulates, named after the 19th century Italian Giuseppe Peano (1858-1932). These axioms define the 'fundamental laws' from which the number system is developed. Peano assumes there are such things as 'numbers' and then defines them in a set of five axioms.

Axioms are the foundations of mathematics. Using what they call 'rules of inferences', mathematicians apply deductive reason to these axioms and create more mathematical knowledge, called theorems. That is the 'mathematical method'. There are no alternative 'mathematical methods'.

Here is a diagrammatic representation of this 'mathematical method':

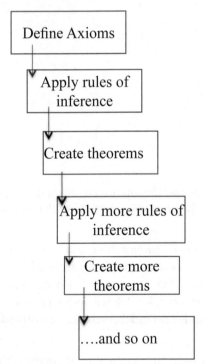

Axioms, rules of inference and theorems

Axioms

Axiomatic knowledge is what philosophers call *a priori* knowledge. *A priori* knowledge is constructed by reasons rather than observation. Most mathematicians claim their axioms are 'self-evident', but this seems simply to be their way of claiming them to be *a priori*. If they are self-evident the very evidence for this must be *a priori* rationalism. Plato was one of the first philosophers to suggest mathematical axioms, and the numbers they use, were *a priori*, although he did not use that term. He saw numbers as belonging to a 'separate and eternal realm' to which humans had a privileged access because of their ability to rationalise.

Rules of Inference

Inference is the forming of conclusions from the information available. Rules of inference therefore, are those rules which mathematicians apply deductively to the mathematical information available to them: axioms. The rules of inference themselves, like axioms, are *a priori*. Rules of inference generate theorems from axioms, and to these new theorems the rules of inference can also be applied.

if... then

A well known rule of inference, one we are all familiar with in some form or other, is the *if... then* rule. Here is a simple example of the *if... then* rule in action.

Arithmetically, *if* $1 + 6 = 7$ and $5 + 4 = 9$
then $(1 + 6) + (5 + 4) = 7 + 9$
or
Algebraically, (algebra is simply arithmetic with variables instead of numbers)
if $x = y$ and $p = q$
then $x + p = y + q$
In bewitching language: equals added to equals are equals. To continue in language rather than numbers or variables, what rules of inference do is imply. That $x = y$ and $p = q$ implies that $x + p = y + q$.

Applying rules of inference deductively to axioms creates new mathematical statements. Each new statement must be consistent with the original axioms, and, use only the original axioms and the new statements generated by the application of the rules of inference. The rules of inference control the process of creating mathematical knowledge in the form of theorems.

Theorems
A theorem is a statement created by deductively applying the rules of inference to axioms. The theorem is presented at the end of the deduction, following the representation of the application of the laws of inference. A theorem is a statement of mathematical knowledge. The process of arriving at it, which has just been described, is the mathematical Way of Knowing.

We all know Pythagoras' Theorem:
...'*The sum of the squares on the arms of a right triangle equals the square on the hypotenuse.*'

This theorem is derived from the 5 Axioms defined in Euclid's Elements. But mathematicians, and budding mathematicians in schools, do not think of Euclid's axioms every time, or even anytime they use it. They take the deductive logic, the application of the rules of inference that arrived at the theorem, as a given. They know they could justify their use of the theorem, but it is not necessary for them to do so.

TOK Ways of Knowing and mathematics

One of the reasons why mathematics is so highly esteemed as an Area of Knowledge is because it is objective. Science, we have seen, is a human construct which strives to be objective, but scientists are aware of the problems of objectivity created by observation and experience-based induction. Mathematics, as an area of knowledge, is free from both observation and induction. The only subjective influence in mathematics would seem to be the mathematician's personal choice of the process of applying the rules of inference: which rules are to be applied, in what order and for what end. As an area of knowledge it demands precise and rigorous *reasoned* intellectual understanding. Despite the fact that most adults do not need more than elementary arithmetical skills in their daily lives, a considerable part of our education is devoted to mathematical knowledge.

It should be clear to you now that mathematics depends on deductive reasoning. Rules of inference are deductive reason. Applying these rules is free from emotion and when language could become a problem mathematicians use their own precise symbols. The big knowledge problems with mathematics are the nature of axioms and where these axioms originate. If, as it has been claimed, axioms are 'established by intuitions which lie too deep for proof' should we just accept them? Is that a priori intuitive knowledge really created by reason?

Mathematics and Sense perception

The mathematical *Way of Knowing* explored in this chapter is the *Way of Knowing* of pure mathematics. No reference has been made to the natural world and it might seem that mathematics has no connection whatsoever with anything other than itself. Applied mathematics, as distinct from pure mathematics, is the use of mathematics in the natural world. Applied mathematics enables humans to construct models of the universe or the trajectory of satellites or the nature of radio waves. This is not mathematics as an area of knowledge as it has been described in this book, rather the use of an area of knowledge to further knowledge in other areas, whether it be physics, economics or even stage design. Perhaps the value of mathematics lies in its ability to be the handmaiden of other *Areas of Knowledge*.

The Language of Mathematics

Many people, mathematicians included, talk about the language of mathematics. We have already defined language as being uniquely human, as communicating and using symbols. Within that definition mathematics is certainly a language. What mathematics communicates in the form of axioms, rules of inference and theorems is restricted, but communicate it certainly does, clearly and precisely,

The symbols of the language of mathematics are as precise as the concepts embedded in them.
= equals = (or more mathematically = = =).

3 = 3.
3 = 2 + 1.
√= √

There is no bewitchment here. Mathematical symbols communicate specific statements that have precise meanings.

A language like this, with carefully defined symbols and rules for using those symbols, is called a *formal language*. Mathematics is a formal language. There is no danger of bewitchment in a formal language. What it communicates it communicates precisely, completely and unambiguously.

The language of mathematics is itself a bewitching phrase. It could mean the formal language of symbols used by mathematicians to communicate precisely with each other. It could be a metaphor for that precision. It could even be a metaphor for the relationships within mathematics. It could mean the specialised use of everyday words within a mathematical context. The formal language of mathematics is a tool perfected by mathematicians to communicate exactly and precisely what they want to communicate. When natural language is used to communicate mathematical ideas the precision of mathematics begins to fade.

Chapter 11

Area of Knowledge 3: The Human Sciences

The Human Sciences

The human sciences are the Areas of Knowledge that study human behaviour, human society and human relationships. The best known of these are:

- *anthropology* (the study of human societies and customs),

- *economics* (the study of the production and distribution of wealth),

- *political science* (the study of the state and systems of government),

- *sociology* (the study of the structure and functioning of human *society)*

- *psychology* (the study of the human mind and its behaviour in specific contexts).

In recent years many colleges and universities have developed degree courses, which use knowledge from the human sciences for specific purposes. For instance, business studies borrow from economics and psychology, and Education courses are composed of, among other things, knowledge from psychology and sociology..

The human sciences are sometimes called the 'social sciences'.

The TOK curriculum planners obviously prefer the word 'human' to 'social'.

Natural science, as you have already seen, is the study of the natural world or the 'phenomena of the physical universe' as philosophers call it. Human beings are certainly a 'phenomena of the physical universe' and human scientists, those scholars who work within the academic disciplines that study the behaviour of human beings, appear to use the same basic method of enquiry as the natural scientists. They observe a selection of 'the phenomena of the natural world'. They use inductive logic to generalise and they create theories that explain and predict. But, despite these apparent similarities of subject matter and method the knowledge generated by human scientists does not have quite the same status as knowledge generated by natural scientists. It is not that knowledge generated by human scientists is not valued, rather that it is valued in a different way. It is regarded rather more as a guideline to what is 'probably' the truth rather than the 'firm' truth of natural science.

Some human scientists resent this. They claim to apply the same standards of objectivity, precision, testability, and reliability as natural scientists; the knowledge they create deserves the same status as knowledge created in the natural sciences. They argue that life would be impossible if people didn't behave in a more or less predictable, measurable way. There are, for example, patterns of behaviour we all follow to obtain social and financial security. Studying human behaviour, they further claim, can help us understand these rules and enables us to generalise about human behaviour in the same way as natural scientists generalise from their observations about other features of the natural world. Of course, they agree, there are exceptions, but in general human behaviour is consistent enough to justify the human sciences as being as objective, precise and testable as any other scientific knowledge. Basically, their view is that human behaviour can be described by a set of rules or laws in much the same way as other aspects of the physical world are described by, for instance, the laws of physics. Human actions, they argue, are simply a division of the phenomena of the natural universe and the action of humans must be governed in the same way as other phenomena.

Despite these claims human science is not quite as reliable, as precise, as objective, and as testable as natural science. Human beings are unique 'phenomena of the physical universe'. But human behaviour, for a whole variety of reasons, is inconsistent and difficult to measure accurately; it is imprecise and subjective. To further complicate matters human scientists are themselves humans; they are part of what they are observing. It is challenging for them to separate their own understanding and awareness of themselves as human beings from the subjects they study. Therefore the methods used to create knowledge in the human sciences are somewhat different from the methods used by natural scientists. To understand the human sciences as a TOK Area of Knowledge we should look at some of those methods.

Observing in the human sciences is not the same as observing in the natural sciences. Considering these problems of observation human scientists have to decide on the appropriate observation methods and data collection techniques using distinct ways of observing. In the diagram (see facing page) showing what, for TOK purposes, I have called the Basic Human Science Method.

As you can see Stages 1, 4, 5 and 6 are the same as the basic scientific method. Stages 2 and 3, focussing on observation, are different.

Five alternative observational techniques are defined: (i) surveys and questionnaires (ii) observations when subjects observed are unaware they are being observed (sometimes called 'in the wild' (iii) controlled experiments, (iv) face-to-face interviews and (v) analysis of existing data. These, of course, are not the only way data is collected but give a sufficient variety to illustrate the observational problems of human scientists. Each technique has its own advantages and disadvantages.

Surveys and questionnaires

Well-designed surveys and questionnaires can, and do, produce accurate data. The two main problems seem to be reliability of the answer (do those completing the survey/questionnaire understand the questions?) and the selection and number of people who respond to the questionnaire.

'In the wild' observation

This too can produce accurate data about people's physical behaviour. You can observe what people *do* but not *why* they do it. Economists observe (the patterns of the rise and fall of prices on the stock exchange). They theorise (when certain conditions are fulfilled prices will drop dramatically). They deduce (these certain conditions are likely to be fulfilled next May). They predict (next May there will be a stock exchange crash). The verification of their prediction (their repeat experiment) takes place in May, when the stock exchange crashes or doesn't crash.

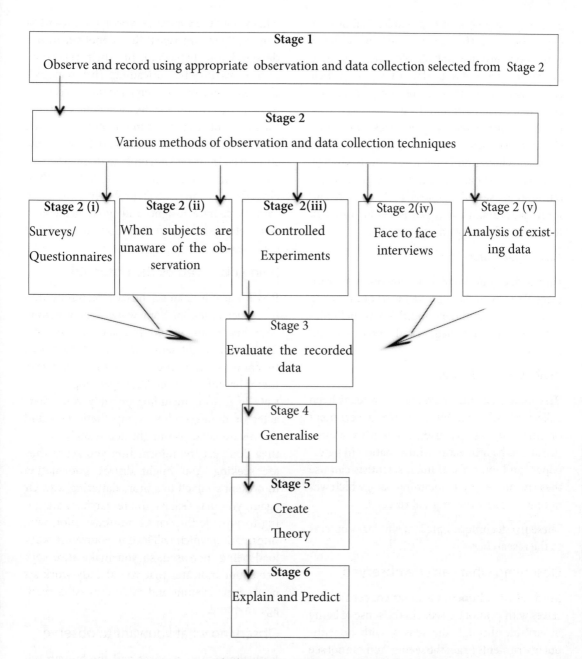

Stage 1

Observe and record using appropriate observation and data collection selected from Stage 2

Stage 2

Various methods of observation and data collection techniques

Stage 2 (i)	**Stage 2 (ii)**	**Stage 2(iii)**	**Stage 2(iv)**	**Stage 2 (v)**
Surveys/ Questionnaires	When subjects are unaware of the observation	Controlled Experiments	Face to face interviews	Analysis of existing data

Stage 3

Evaluate the recorded data

Stage 4

Generalise

Stage 5

Create

Theory

Stage 6

Explain and Predict

The 'Basic Human Science Method'

Controlled Experiments

Observation in the natural sciences often means experimenting. The replication of the experiment, confirming the knowledge generated by previous experiments, is the test that natural scientific knowledge has to pass. In the human sciences this kind of experiment is impossible. Controlled experiments with very small groups of people, experiments, which concentrate on all possible variables, are extremely difficult to run. Could research into attitudes to homework in any one class in your school or college be replicated? It might indicate attitudes for that particular group at that particular time, and these attitudes might reflect more general attitudes throughout the school or college or even schools and colleges generally. But replication in the rigorous sense of the natural science experiment is not possible. 'Laboratory experiments' in the human sciences are faced with too many uncontrollable variables. People change from day to day: they worry, their cars break down, their crops don't grow, they get excited, they get bored. People change over time: they get older, they get backaches, their children don't do their homework. And groups of people change and therefore cultures change. Compare your parents' and your grandparents' attitudes to sex, drugs and rock 'n' roll, and footwear. Human behaviour is too inconsistent to be part of controlled experiments.

Face-to-face interviews

Face-to-face interviews have obvious disadvantages. The researcher can adapt the questions to ensure they are understood. Non-verbal clues including body language can be observed and recorded.

Analysis of existing data.

Researchers examine data that has already been collected and is readily available: government or other surveys, censuses, tax returns, educational and health records, information in newspapers and journals. Human scientists can use these resources often obtaining data, which was not intended by the original research.

These five techniques present similar problems to the researcher.

Observing what can't be observed

Much of what human scientists concern themselves with cannot be 'seen', in the sense of being observable through the senses, with or without instruments to aid the seeing. You cannot see 'motivation' or 'leadership' or 'concentration'.

To understand these, and the many similar characteristics of human behaviour, human scientists have to rely on their own 'empathy and introspection', rather like the proverbial 'sixth sense'. Why didn't you attend class yesterday? Were you lazy? Ill? Bored? Otherwise engaged? Rebellious? Doing your own thing? Human scientists cannot be sure of your reason for being absent (they can ask you of course, but

what would the answer be worth?) so they must consult their own repertoire of motives to understand your behaviour. But their 'repertoire of motives' may be misleading. They may pick the wrong one or not even have the correct one in their repertoire. Or the behaviour may be a blend of motives that are impossible to separate from each other. Human scientists can make some well informed attempts to define the reason you were not in class yesterday and their empathetic analysis will probably give them some accurate insights into your behaviour. But *probably* is not *definitely*. You can't see what can't be seen.

Being observed by the observed

If you knew human scientists researching into the effectiveness of homework were watching your behaviour, would you act entirely normally? You might sense what it is they hoped to know (even if you were wrong) and give them that information. Or, depending on a variety of factors, including possibly your character or mood, or how sympathetic you find the researchers, you might deliberately ensure they don't get the information you sense they are seeking. You might distort information to present yourself in a more flattering way. Or again, you may believe the researchers are going to provide the school administration with information which will lead to your homework load being increased, so you make sure your behaviour indicates that you already work six hours every evening and couldn't possible manage anymore.

Observing what youwant to observe

Both the natural sciences and the human sciences are human constructs. These humans who construct them have values, values that classify actions and achievements, goals and aspirations, as good or bad, just or unjust, worthy or worthless. Any personal values or biases that scientists, natural or human, bring to their research should be made explicit and compensated for. Physicists looking for an all-embracing Theory of Everything must be extremely careful that their desire to find such a theory doesn't interfere with their observations and deductions. Human scientists face the same kind of problems as physicists. But, their researches are even more vulnerable to personal values because they, the human scientists, are themselves human and part of their own subject matter. Human scientists researching the effectiveness of homework have themselves experienced homework. Their own experience may lead them to believe that homework is fundamental to success later in life or that it is simply a device used to keep young people busy and to control them or train them to work hard or one of a thousand other things. They may make their values explicit and compensate for them, may even overcompensate, but it is impossible for them to ignore them completely. Total, value-free objectivity is not possible in either natural or human science. But, in human science it is more difficult to achieve than in natural science. Seeing what you want to see distorts.

The Hawthorne Effect

Aware as they are of the possible problems, human scientists do, nevertheless, attempt laboratory type tests. A well-known example of such a test took place at the Western Electrical Company's factory in Hawthorne in California. The management were concerned about efficiency, so they hired a team of human scientists to investigate the effects of changing working conditions on productivity and morale. A group of workers was installed in an assembly line in a room separated from the main assembly line. In this separate room variations in working conditions could be altered and carefully monitored. The researchers changed certain working conditions, for instance the level of lighting and the frequency of breaks, but changed only one variable at a time, in the best experimental tradition. The results at first seem self-evident: the better the lighting or the more breaks, the 'better' the working environment, the higher the morale and productivity. But then the researchers 'dis-improved' the environment: lower levels of lighting and fewer breaks, and still the productivity improved. Morale and productivity, it was concluded, increased because the workers were singled out for attention: a consequence now known generally as the Hawthorne Effect. The Hawthorne Experiment indicates a major difficulty with 'laboratory' experimenting in the human sciences: the problem of the observers being observed by the observed.

TOK Ways of Knowing

TOK's *Ways of Knowing*, sense perception, reason, emotion and language are all involved in the creation of knowledge in the human sciences. The complication for the Human Sciences is that the emotion of the researchers inevitably affects their reason when interpreting sense perception data. To what extent their reason is affected will depend on many factors. Language is used to both create and communicate findings. An obvious TOK knowledge issue, for instance, is *To what extent the language of questionnaires and surveys and interviews affect the data produced by them?*

The search for perfection

Human scientists are aware of the imperfections of human science as an Area of Knowledge. For this reason they constantly appraise the methods they use. They are particularly interested in distinguishing the human sciences from what is known as 'human lore', the kind of traditional common sense beliefs about a society and how it works, which members of a particular society hold. Human science, they claim, is different from human lore for three main reasons:

- Human science is an 'explanatory enterprise of culturally *universal* validity'. The important word here is 'universal'. If the human sciences do give 'universal' explanations of human behaviour then it would be significantly different from human lore.

- Human science is an 'explanatory enterprise that is interpretively neutral'. Human science is not subjective and human scientists are neutral when they report and interpret human behaviour.

- Human science is an 'explanatory enterprise which is evaluatively independent.' Human science looks at human behaviour and explains it without judging.

TOK aims to get you thinking critically about such statements. The difference between human science and natural science is a basic TOK knowledge issue.

Chapter 12

Areas of Knowledge 4 : History

History is the study of the human past. The word 'history' comes from the Greek 'historia', which means 'inquiry, knowledge acquired by investigation'. In TOK we need to understand the nature of that 'investigation'. The TOK guide makes it quite clear that history is not a scientific investigation. Would be 'knowers' of history, historians, cannot *directly observe* the past and therefore cannot be classified as scientists. Knowledge in history is, at best, second hand. This makes historical investigation, the creation of new history, quite distinct from other *Areas of Knowledge*.

A nineteenth century German historian, Ranke, used the phrase 'wie es eigentlich gewesen' ('how it really was') to describe how he believed historians should present their records of the past. Ranke and his fellow nineteenth century historians believed that not only was it possible to present the past 'how it really was' but they also believed they were doing exactly that when they wrote their history books. They regarded history as they regarded the natural sciences. There are, they claimed, 'historical' facts just as there are 'scientific' facts. In the same way that scientific facts were independent of the scientists, so historical facts were regarded as independent of the historian. The historian's job was to collect together a proven body of facts and present them.

Modern historians regard this approach not only as impossibly idealistic but also as simply impossible. Why? Isn't that what history is about? What is history if it is not about the facts of the past? If it isn't the past 'wie es eigentlich gewesen'?

We all know, or think we know, what a 'fact' is: a reliable piece of information, something we know to be, in the common sense meaning of the word 'true'. We also know, or think we know, what a historical fact is. We can produce, without too much trouble, at least half a dozen historical facts: the date of Nelson Mandela's release from prison, the year the French revolutionaries stormed the Bastille, the number of times Brazil has won the World (Soccer) Cup, the year of Tut Ankh Amon's death, the name of the Chinese communist ruler responsible for the purges in the 1960s, and so on. These are facts, definite pieces of historical knowledge.

These 'facts', these pieces of evidence about the human past, are important to historians. Historians collect their evidence from wherever they can and must be certain of their accuracy. Certain historical facts, often obtained from archives, may be collected directly. Historians can visit public record offices and examine historical documents personally. Historians sometimes interview people who were directly connected with the historical events they are researching and obtain 'oral' history. Other historical evidence is obtained from the academic disciplines, which underpin history, subjects like archaeology, palaeontology, numismatology, and so on.

Epigraphy is an interesting example of such a discipline. This is the study of ancient inscriptions: letters and words and symbols, chiselled, moulded or embossed on stones, metal, clay, even wood. These inscriptions and their interpretation by epigraphists provide some of the basic factual evidence for historians.

But factual evidence is only the start of history. History is the processing of this evidence into a coherent narrative with causes and effects. Historians write in the context of their own time and are inevitably influenced in their interpretation by their own motivation, ideas and values as well as the ideas and values of those who will read their work. All history, it has been forcefully argued by an Italian historian Benedetto Croce, is contemporary history.

ment: maps, treaties, church and temple records, imperial archive documents, letters, legal records, diaries, newspapers, catalogues and even bus tickets. They can be formal or informal, private or public, serious or frivolous. Primary sources also include *artefacts*. The underground bunkers in Whitehall, London from which Churchill ran his wartime government are a wonderful primary source, as are the pyramids in south America, the Great Wall of

The history l *Area of Knowledge* is constructed something like this:

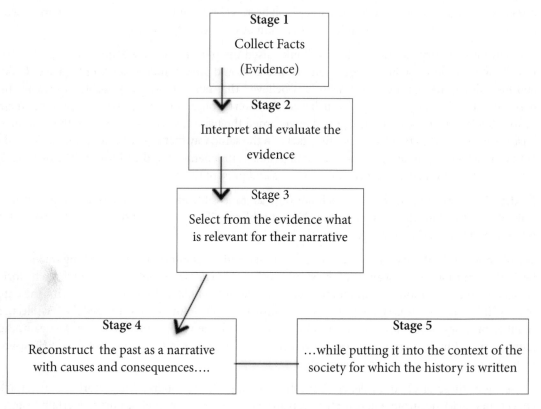

Stage 1

Collect Facts

(Evidence)

Stage 2

Interpret and evaluate the evidence

Stage 3

Select from the evidence what is relevant for their narrative

Stage 4

Reconstruct the past as a narrative with causes and consequences….

Stage 5

…while putting it into the context of the society for which the history is written

Stage 1. Collect Facts (Evidence)

Primary and Secondary Sources

The problem with the past is that it has passed. It has gone. It can't be observed and it can't be verified by further observation, We have to explore the past through what remains: through the multitude of surviving artefacts. Historians use what they term 'primary sources' as their main access to the past.

Primary sources are the foundations of history. They include every conceivable type of docu-

China, cave paintings in central France and stone sculptures on the Easter Islands.

'Secondary sources' are also used: these are sources of information provided by other historians. Gibbon's *Decline and Fall of the Roman Empire*, written in the eighteenth century, is a secondary source. It is Gibbon's account of the end of the Roman Empire, written almost two thousand years after the event(s). It describes and analyses. In contrast, Julius Caesar's *The Gallic Wars* is a primary source: Caesar actually was there, fighting those wars. Other secondary sources might not be so obvious: the novel *Huckleberry Finn* is a much used secondary source used by historians writing about slavery in the United States in the nineteenth century, even though it is a work of fiction.

Stage 2. Interpret and evaluate the evidence

Information from both primary and secondary sources needs to be treated with great caution.

Can historians be sure they understand the meaning of any evidence as it was originally intended? If it is a document do the actual words mean what they seem to mean? If the language used has to be translated has the bias of the translator, however subconscious, affected the interpretation? Historians attempt to overcome these problems by using as many varied primary sources as possible.

Historians are wary of all sources and here are some of the questions they ask when using primary (and secondary) sources:

- Who produced this source?

- When was it produced?

- Was the creator of the source an eyewitness?

- Why was the source produced?

- Where was the source produced?

- Is there consistency within the source?

- Is there consistency with other sources?

All these questions are aspects of one main question: how reliable is this source? Historians approach sources attempting to imaginatively understand—not necessarily to sympathise with—the minds of the creators of the documents. Imaginative understanding is an important part of a historian's skill, but varies from historian to historian. Can modern historians, coming with their own prejudices and biases, reliably process information from the past, process it not only aware of the intentions of the creators of the document but also fully aware of the biases and prejudices of the generation to which they themselves belong? Is there any way in which modern historians can guarantee their freedom from bias or prejudice or expectation? Would Japanese historians be able to interpret European feudalism without being influenced by their understanding of the similar social systems in Japan?

Historians need to put their primary sources into their context. Primary sources need careful evaluation. They might tell (a) what the writer(s) genuinely thought had happened or was happening, or (b) what the writer(s) wanted others to think they thought, or even (c) what the writer(s) thought ought to have happened. A well-known example of this is the 'fact' that common people, the 'peasants' in Medieval Europe were devout Christians. What evidence we have for this comes, of course, from the people in the Middle Ages who wrote about their own lives and times. And the people who wrote about their own lives and times in the Middle Ages in Europe were monks and priests. Were these people capable of being objective about something so important to them as their religion?

Stage 3. Select from the evidence what is relevant for your narrative

Having interpreted and evaluated the evidence historians then have the task of selecting which 'facts' are to be used in their histories. Historians select, but what they select inevitably reflects the perspective of the audience for whom they write. When the histories of the 'Arab Spring' revolutions in north Africa in 2011 come to be written those historians seeking to explain to the Chinese will write a quite different story from those historians writing to influence American foreign policy. Historians who feel strongly about the spread of democracy will write a different narrative from those whose values are underpinned by religion. Other historians will write history to earn a living or increase their status in an academic community. The material they select for instance to explain the downfall of aging dictators may be 'true' but will be a selection of the truth appealing to a particular audience. Historians select, but what they select reflects the reason they are writing the history and the audience for whom they are writing.

Stage 4. Reconstructing the past as a narrative with causes and consequences

History is not a portrait of the past, nor historians' thoughts about the past, but the bringing together of these two things. The task of the historian is to create a narrative, to write a 'story' from his selected evidence, a story describing human activity in the past and analysing the cause and consequences of these human actions. Out of this will come the narrative, a tale of events and motivations, actions, successes, failures, aspirations and all the other human activities.

Stage 5. Put into context of the society for which the history is written

Historians also put their conclusions into some kind of context. They ask themselves questions about the relevance of their findings and conclusions to other contexts. What, if anything, can conclusions tell us about human communities in general? They might compare the artefacts from one culture to the artefacts found in another. Historians often compare and contrast human behaviour from the past with contemporary human behaviour. Historians continually reinterpret the events of the past and reappraise them for each new generation.

An example: the life of the 20th Century Ugandan President Idi Amin

If an historian were to write a history of the life of the Ugandan leader Idi Amin, who ruled Uganda from 1971 to 1979, his or her work might develop like this:

Stage one. Collect the facts (Evidence)

Obviously the researcher would have find out as much as possible about Amin. He or she would have to read all the published material about Amin, would have to visit the government archives in Uganda to see records of government proceedings and in other countries that had dealings with him, obtain facsimiles of newspaper and other contemporary accounts of events, speak to people who knew Amin and worked with him, and so on and so on , finding out as much about him and his actions and attitudes as possible.

Stage Two. Interpret and evaluate the evidence

Of course with a subject like Amin the researcher could never read everything and would at some time have to say, enough, now I have an immense amount of information, which of this information is really reliable? Which tells me something about Amin that is important? Is there information here that is plainly biased? Is there information here that is clearly a true and accurate account of the events described? The historian has to make judgements about these things.

Stage Three. Select from the evidence what is relevant.

At this point the motive and perspective of the historian is important. The researcher will have some idea of the emphasis and perspective of the history. What is the purpose of the research and who will be the intended audience? If it is intended for the general reader is it possible that material may be selected because it will improve sales of the book? Whatever the motive, selection is inevitable. The writer has to decide on his or her perspective: was, for instance Amin a victim of the times he lived in or was he responsible for his actions?

Stage Four. Reconstruct the past as a narrative with causes and effect.

Having decided on the material to be used the historian then puts together an account of Amin's life, possibly starting with his childhood and early military career and presumably trying to define certain strands and developments which enable the reader to get a clear picture of his way of life, his attitudes and motivations, his political and social values, what caused him to be the person he was. Certain key events, presumably his career in the colonial army, his coming to power, his tyrannical rule, his speech at the United Nations and final overthrow, will be described.

Stage Five. Put into context

This last step will attempt to put Amin in some sort of historical and geographical context. The political, social and economic state not only of Uganda, but of eastern and central Africa at the time will be considered. Another important consideration will be the effect of Amin's rule. What is the legacy of his years in power?

History and the TOK diagram

In TOK students are expected to come to some understanding of what *Ways of Knowing*, selected from sense perception, reason, language and emotion, historians use to create history.

In Stage 1, collecting evidence, there is obviously considerable use of *sense perception*. Historians use their senses to study artefacts and documents. The difference between them and natural and human scientists, as we have already seen, is the nature of the material they perceive.

In stage 2, interpreting and evaluating the evidence, *reason* and *language* become important but so also does imagination. Historians have to use their imagination to recreate the purpose of artefacts, the motivation of the people creating them, the reliability and built-in bias of primary sources. Is this imaginative projection *reason* or *emotion*?

In Stage 3 historians select evidence relevant to their narrative. Reason must be significant in this process but again emotion must be involved. Selection can be motivated by values and attitudes that are embedded into a society often without the society being aware they are.

In Stage 4, reconstructing the past as a narrative, language is important, as language is the medium with which the past is presented and the choice of words and they way the past is presented can influences that reconstruction.

The final stage 5, the assumptions the historian is making about the society for which the history is written are as emotional as they are reasoned. Generalising about the use of the TOK *Ways of Knowing* is always a little difficult. As a TOK student you should be prepared to look at each 'bit' of history you encounter and bring your awareness of the way history is created to critically examine it.

Historians themselves are keen to debate the nature of their discipline and have suggested many reasons for the study of history. Here, selected from the comments of historians, are some of them. It will help your understanding of the nature of the subject if you put these in some order of importance for (a) yourself (b) your grandparents (c) your history teacher and (d) the chief political leader of your country.

History makes people patriotic. History is an intellectual pursuit in itself, an activity of the reasoning mind.

Societies need to know and understand their past. History helps us to understand the present.

History explains why things happen. History teaches us about human behaviour. The history of other countries makes us more tolerant. History provides a pleasurable leisure time activity.

Chapter 13

Areas of Knowledge 5: The Arts

The arts comprise a huge range of human creative activity. They include painting, sculpture, ceramics, architecture, music, dance, film, and all the many genres of literature. For TOK purposes it is helpful to restrict our discussion to the conventional school subjects of literature, art and music. In your A1 language literature classes you read novels and discuss the ideas embedded in them. In your art classes you create your own art and look at paintings and sculptures by famous artists, and discuss their intent and impact. In music you make music and listen to music from all parts of the world .

Both science and art organise reality. The 'reality' of science is the natural world organised rationally through our sense perception. The 'reality' of art is the reality of our experience as emotional humans organised in such a way that we can communicate it to others. The knowledge of art is knowledge acquired by our ability to understand our fellow humans' emotions, our ability to *empathise*. Empathy is to the artist what sense perception is to the scientist.

The 19th century Russian Writer Leo Tolstoy, a serious artist himself, defined art's way of knowing in a way appropriate for TOK:

> To evoke in oneself a feeling one has experienced, and having evoked it in oneself, then, by means of movements, lines, colours, sound or forms, expressed in words, so to transmit that feeling that others may experience the same feeling—that is the activity of art. Art is a human activity, consisting in this, that one man consciously, by means of certain external signs, hands on to others feelings he has lived through, and that other people are infected by these feelings, and also experience them.

Tolstoy has not focussed on how the artist obtains the experience that has created the feeling he evokes. In TOK diagram terms that experience begins with sense perception, the same sense perception that creates knowledge in the natural and human sciences. Artists observe the world about them; they see, hear, touch, taste and smell the world they live in. They observe the way people behave and they respond to that behaviour sometimes with emotion, sometimes with reason, often with a mixture of both and they create Tolstoy's 'feeling that one has experienced'. The thing that artists do (that scientists do not do) is to bring their own response, their own emotional instincts and values, to the creation of that 'feeling'. The knowledge issue is to determine the origin and value, the 'truth', of those emotional instincts and values.

Count Leo Tolstoy 1828-1910: Russian landowner and writer whose works include *War and Peace* (considered by many to be the greatest novel ever written), *Anna Karenina* and *Death of Ivan Ulich*. He spent the last years of his life in voluntary poverty, living as a peasant, having given his estate to his family and disposed of all his possessions. In 1901 the Russian Orthodox Church excommunicated him because of his hostility to their practices. His description of art, quoted on p.75 is taken from his work *What is Art?* - published in 1898.

To reduce art as a way-of-knowing to a diagram is inviting scorn from philosophers, but for those of you who are uncertain what Tolstoy is saying, here it is:

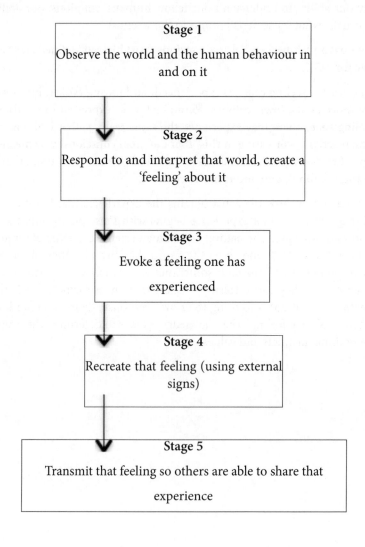

Stage 1
Observe the world and the human behaviour in and on it

Stage 2
Respond to and interpret that world, create a 'feeling' about it

Stage 3
Evoke a feeling one has experienced

Stage 4
Recreate that feeling (using external signs)

Stage 5
Transmit that feeling so others are able to share that experience

Stage 1. Observe the world and human behaviour in and on it.

Artists are free to observe any thing. They can look at the sea, at tsunamis, at mountains, at desserts, at animals and birds and their fellow humans. They can even leave their physical world and observe the universe

Stage 2 Respond to and interpret that world, create a feeling about it.

The artists' personal responses and interpretations can be totally unrestricted. They can use their emotions and their reason and their self awareness to explain their responses to the detail of an insect's wing case, the need a child has for parental love, the obsessive greed of some members of society, the problems that lead people to war or murder, the pains and pleasure of love, of frustration, of ambition, of corruption. This feeling can arise from artists' exceptional imagination and intellect, their ability to understand and interpret the world and the people who live in it in a personal and often profound way.

Stage 3 Evoke a feeling one has experienced

'Evoke' here means to recall and to bring it to the centre of your thoughts, your consciousness, to make it the focal point of your interest and to feel it with clarity and intensity.

Stage 4 Recreate that feeling

What distinguishes great artists is not only the quality, the 'truth' of their feelings, but also their ability to manipulate what Tolstoy calls 'external signs' to transmit that truth. Great artists are great because their ability to recreate understanding with their chosen signs, be these signs in paint, marble, words, music or movement, is outstanding.

Stage 5 Transmit that feeling so others are able to share that experience

The experience of the artist becomes an experience for the artist's audience, reader, viewer and listener when the audience share the feeling created. The artist has evoked something to share. For this reason one can argue that art is not a matter of personal response. If your response to a work of art is not the feeling that the artist evoked (Stage 3) then the artist has failed. You may not like the feeling evoked that the artist has recreated in you, a feeling readers, viewers or listeners may respond to in different ways.

What the artist knows...

From *The Meaning of Art* Herbert Read 1972

The artist pours his knowledge into works of art. He knows—he does not merely feel—but he knows by sympathetic identification and imaginative insight. He knows as the perspicacious lover knows about the nature of love, by 'proving it upon his pulses' He knows by feeling at one with the object, as Keats felt at one with the sparrow. He knows the reality that he suffers when the outer object is drawn into his own being, into the mysterious depths of subjectivity. He knows not bare facts or abstract laws but vivid values —he knows things appreciatively, in their immediacy and concreteness. He knows with the totality of his body: with sense, mood, instinct, and intelligence, both conscious and subconscious. He knows by descending to the roots of being, which no idea can encompass—to the obscure spring of man's creative intuition—the source of dreams and of art alike. There, in the deep recesses of his mind, he is in touch with the instinctively common part of man's nature—with the values that are not peculiar to him as an artist, not to one man or a few, but are basic in the emotional experiences and secret longings of most human beings. If it were not so, art could not serve as the language of all humanity—a way of communicating across all the barriers of place and time. The cave paintings by men of the reindeer age— the paintings at Lascaux and Altamira—would not speak so eloquently to us today; nor would the art of the whole world be a 'museum without walls' where any man can find incomparable treasures. The work of all ages and countries— Gothic counterpoint, Egyptian sculpture, Chinese landscape, Mayan temple, Russian ballet, English drama, and American novel— bear alike the spiritual imprint of humanity. In the realm of art, far more than in morals, politics, or religion, the whole world is kin.

Area of Knowledge or area of experience?

Because the arts, as an Area of Knowledge, depend on creativity and individual insights, it has been suggested that it is an area of *experience* rather than an area of *knowledge*. Within Tolstoy's definition a case can be made that knowledge—his 'feeling'—is generated and transmitted. Whether you call the arts an *Area of knowledge* or an *Area of experience* depends on your understanding of what you mean by 'knowledge' and what it is 'to know'.

The knowledge within the arts, based on the evocation of feelings, is not the justified true belief of Plato (see Chapter 15). Plato was hostile to art. For him it was a rival to the pursuit of truth and had the potential to corrupt. It is not difficult to have sympathy for the pragmatic Plato. The 'truth' of the arts cannot be put into words. It is difficult to explain adequately the 'feelings'

people experience when reading a novel, listening to music or looking at art

Art as an area of knowledge: Literature

'Literature' is one of those bewitching words that can mean many things. In the context of the arts as an area of knowledge it means poetry, drama, novels and short stories, works of art created with language by individual poets, playwrights and novelists. The kind of material you study in Language A1. Here is an example of literature, a short poem by a distinguished Nigerian writer.

Refugee Mother and Child

No Madonna and Child could touch
that picture of a mother's tenderness
for a son she soon would have to forget.

The air was heavy with odours
of diarrhoea of unwashed children
with washed out ribs and dried-up

bottoms struggling in laboured
steps behind blown empty bellies.
Most mothers there had long ceased
to care but not this one; she held
a ghost smile between her teeth
and in her eyes the ghost of a mother's
pride as she combed the rust-coloured
hair left on his skull and then -
singing in her - began carefully
to part it...In another life this
would have been a little daily
act of no consequence before his
breakfast and school; now she
did it like putting flowers
on a tiny grave.

Chinua Achebe

Achebe has done exactly what Tolstoy claims artists do. He has observed an incident in a refugee camp (Stage 1) and the feeling he experienced there (Stage 2), evoked the incident he saw directly and his compassionate response indirectly (Stage 3), has re-created that incident and his feeling with external signs (Stage 4) in this case words, transmitted that feeling to others and recreated that it so others share that experience (Stage 5).

Perhaps you are thinking, that's fine for this short emotional poem but how can a novel, *Huckleberry Finn* for example, possibly recall a 'feeling' that Mark Twain had experienced? The answer to that question is simple. *Huckleberry Finn* recalls not one feeling but a multitude of feelings that Mark Twain had about, amongst other things, the pains and pleasures of childhood, hypocrisy and pretence, and the values of the people who lived on and along the Mississippi River in the mid nineteenth century. His 'external symbols'— the extended prose narrative, the choice of Huck, a 14 year old, as narrator, the selection of events—determine the effectiveness of the recreation and transmission of Mark Twain's feelings. That *Huckleberry Finn* has been read and enjoyed for over a century, and continues to be widely read in the 21st

century is proof of the quality of the 'medium' of the novel as well as its 'message.'

A problem some people find in reading literature is the problem of accepting the message that is transmitted. If you are not able to accept the 'truth' of literature then it has failed as literature. Mark Twain doesn't openly list the pains and pleasures of childhood, his feeling, his truth, comes from the convincing way in which he presents Huck and his values, displaying the truth rather than explaining it. If Huck is not convincing then the reader will not accept the truth on which his portrayal is based

This 'convincingness' leads to another problem some people have with literature: how can you be convinced by something you know doesn't exist? Huck is a character in a book. He is an imaginary person, a product of Mark Twain's imagination, they argue. You can only be convinced by him if you are prepared to be imaginative too. Literature demands the reader uses imagination. Imaginative involvement in literature can take us into a whole range of awareness that is not otherwise easily accessible or might even be dangerous. We can suffer with Huck in his relationship with his father. We can savour the grandeur and power of the river. We can comprehend the bitterness and the folly of family feuds. Our imaginative involvement is caused by the skill of the writer in creating, through external signs, the situation in which we willingly suspend our disbelief.

Imagination is the power of the mind to create images of things, which are not present, and to relate to images of things that are not real. Imagination could be described as creative thought. When we are creatively thinking—imagining—when we are drifting down the Mississippi with Huck, we are not deluding ourselves. We know our imaginary experience is not real. When we read literature our imagination is brought into action by the feelings and external symbols of the writer creating images in our minds. We 'see' the waves ripple on the surface of the water and we 'see' the paddle boat, belching smoke, steaming up the centre of the river. When writers present us with events or people that we cannot accept, that our imaginations can't process, either our imagination, or the writer, has failed

Art as an area of knowledge : The Visual Arts

The great palaces of the world—The Imperial Palaces of the Forbidden City in Beijing, the Topkapi Palace in Istanbul, the Palace of Versailles in France, are famous examples of the visual arts; clearly illustrating Tolstoy's definition of art as a Way of Knowing. All three create a definite feeling about the power and status of the dynastic families that commissioned and owned them, and the feelings the architects had when they designed them. By the use of external symbols —stone, glass, wood, space, trees —the architects of these palaces transmit the 'truth' of the wealth and opulence and power of the great ruling families. In the same way 'the glory of God' is transmitted through the architecture of the great mosques, temples and cathedrals throughout the world.

The architects of the palaces have created, through their art, their feeling of power and glory. If their art is successful they have communicated that feeling. We do not have to agree with their feeling to appreciate the 'truth' of their art. We can admire the 'external symbols' easily, the design and shape of the buildings, the craftsmanship by which art is constructed. But we also visit the Imperial Palace to sense the glory and power of the Chinese Emperors, however much we may regard them as despotic tyrants.

This ability to communicate feeling applies to the other visual arts, even though these may lack the grandeur of great architecture. A Persian miniature can convey the excitement of a hunt, and a French impressionist the delight of a garden, as a cathedral displays the glory of God. Abstract art, which developed in the 1940s and 1950s, is as much *art* in Tolstoy's definition as the more conventional art of the cathedral architects and the French impressionists. By eliminating recognisable figures and objects, artists are free to express their feelings with abstract lines, colours and shapes.

Wasily Kandinsky (1866-1944), a pioneer abstract painter produced in his paintings 'the choir of colours which nature has so painfully thrust into my soul'. Painting was for him 'an exact replica of an inner emotion'.

Art as an area of knowledge : Music

Music is the simplest of the arts to relate to our interpretation of Tolstoy's construction of an Area of Knowledge. Anyone who has attended an American major league baseball game knows what knowledge is transmitted through music. Just before the game begins, the guest singer walks to the diamond, the spectators rise and with hands on their hearts join together to sing *The Star Spangled Banner*. Everyone in the stadium is, for that moment, part of a confident, united nation: 'the land of the free and the home of the brave'. Patriotism, pride in one's country, fills the ballpark. You can feel the stars and stripes rising above the stadium, spreading the message of freedom and confidence.

The Star Spangled Banner makes its statement with clarity: its external symbols, the musical sounds, evoke the composer's feeling of patriotism and recreate that feeling within those baseball fans. The musical message in this case is far from subtle but it is certainly powerful in a style that no language can be.

Beethoven was convinced of the power of music as an area of knowledge. 'Music', he said, 'is a higher revelation than all wisdom and philosophy.' He claimed it was 'an entrance into the higher world of knowledge which comprehends mankind but which mankind cannot comprehend.' He stated also it was 'the mediator between the intellectual and the sensuous life'.

Music expresses mood and atmosphere— serenity, exuberance, anticipation, triumph, sadness, fury and much else—in a way language cannot. Movie makers claim that music is responsible for 80% of the emotional impact of their work. More important than these definable moods and atmospheres is the power of music to express feelings which can only be expressed, and transmitted, through music itself.

Feelings for which there are no words. Great music is alive: it creates indefinable feelings that change as you become increasingly familiar with it and feelings of which you never tire.

Not all music, not all art, is great and timeless. Popular music, as it is called, the music of the charts, is hypnotic, entertaining and temporary. Alan Bloom, a distinguished American political philosopher has this to say about rock music in particular:

...(there) are the three great lyrical themes (of rock music): sex, hate and a smarmy, hypocritical version of brotherly love... A glance at the videos that project images on the wall of Plato's cave since MTV took it over suffices to prove this.. .... Nothing noble, sublime, profound, delicate, tasteful or even decent can find a place in such a tableaux. There is room only for the intense, changing, crude and immediate...

If it does nothing else this tirade confirms the power of music.

The Arts and the TOK diagram

In TOK diagram terms Achebe's knowledge starts with his *sense perception*, what he observed in the refugee camp. His sense perception is filtered through *emotion*, his compassion for the mother and child and to some extent *reason,* his comparison with alternatives, and is dependent on *language* both to construct and transmit the 'knowledge'.

The visual arts have one advantage over literature, an advantage they share with music: they are free from the bewitchment of language. The knowledge generated by the visual arts is wordless. The medieval architects' feeling for the glory of God expressed and transmitted through great cathedrals transcends any attempt to put this feeling into words. Words, as symbols, we already know, create a barrier to our knowing. Visual art, in a metaphorical sense, creates its own language. The external symbols used by artists, the paint, the canvas, the marble, the bricks and mortar, become the language, and on the skill of the artist in manipulating this language depends, partially, the success of the art. 'Partially' is important here. If the knowledge is not worth transmitting no amount of artistic skill in the manipulation of the external symbols will make it so.

Chapter 14

Area of Knowledge 6: Ethics

Ethics, the study of human morality, is the odd-man-out on the TOK diagram outer circle. The other five Areas of Knowledge are all conventional school and diploma subjects. In the Diploma hexagon, Part 3, individuals and society, philosophy is an option and ethics is an option within that option. Inevitably very few Diploma students come into direct contact with ethics other than in TOK.

A curriculum for senior/high schools, for students about to enter universities or work, which does not introduce students to distinctions between right and wrong and the justification of moral judgments is missing an important Area of Knowledge. The Diploma programme needs ethics. It may fit a little uncomfortably into TOK, but there it is. The TOK perspective is not to teach ethics, but to look at how ethical knowledge is constructed and to encourage students to be aware of their own ethical values. TOK examines the sources of ethical knowledge - reason, emotion, sense, perception, language, and prepares students to critically think about those sources and their own responsibility for moral actions. TOK looks at the way ethical knowledge is created, not at the ethics itself.

Most of us are brought up to follow certain ethical rules, to behave in ways which are considered acceptable by the society in which we live. Here are some examples of ethical rules that different groups of people have followed at some time or another.

- Never take a human life.

- Never cause needless pain or suffering.

- Do not gamble.

- Do not drink alcoholic drinks.

- Do not eat pork.

- Do not steal.

- Never tell a lie.

Each rule states what not to do but it doesn't give reasons. These rules do not tell us the ethical principles on which they are based.

In the past there was considerable agreement that religion, in the form of the commands of god or gods, determined right or wrong. The faith based edicts of Moses, Jesus, Mohammed, Buddha and Hindu gods, amongst many others, defined the moral structure of societies.

In contrast, from the time of the ancient Greeks, moral philosophers have been attempting to define ethical principles acceptable to all independent of their faith or lack of faith. So leaving aside religious theories this chapter attempts to understand the nature of ethical knowledge. It examines the ethical theories of three notable philosophers, Aristotle, Kant and Rand; and their explanations of the principles on which they are based. Of course there are many philosophers who have thought about ethics. These three have been selected because they cover a wide time band from the 4th century BC until 20th century US and because they all attempt to articulate their ideas in an accessible manner.

Aristotle (384 BC-322 BC)

Self-interest

In his incomplete and condensed lecture notes Aristotle defined what has become known as the Self-Interest ethical theory. He asserts the difference between humans and all other living forms is that humans are rational, reasoning beings. The concepts of right and wrong, of virtue and vice, he claims are an intrinsic part of human rationality. Aristotle also maintained that, as part of our human rationality, we strive to lead a successful life. We all seek what he calls *eudaimonia*. (Classical scholars say *eudaimonia* is a difficult word to translate. Sometimes it is translated as happiness but it seems to mean more than that, something *like being content with life in a fulfilled and virtuous way*.) Good humans, 'good' in an ethical sense, take pleasure in being virtuous and this virtuousness leads to eudaimonia. It is in our own self-interest to rationally cultivate virtues like generosity, bravery, temperance and loyalty because the long-term practice of such virtues leads us into a state of eudaimonia.

Supporters of self-interest ethics argue strongly that self-interest is not selfishness. Concern for others is not only compatible with self-interest—it is basic to it. Concern for others is *reasoned* self-interest. To help others is to help oneself. If you rob banks to obtain money to 'do your own thing' sooner or later you will end up in prison and in the meantime spend a lot of emotional energy worrying about being caught. Being in prison or worrying about being put into in prison is not in your own long-term self-interest. People in prison want to get out

Aristotle has no doubt: the concepts of right and wrong are an intrinsic part of our rationality. Reason, he claims, intrinsic reason, is where

our morality comes from. Reduced to its basics here is Aristotle's argument.

Premise1.Humans are rational

Premise 2. Knowing what is morally right and wrong, good and bad, is intrinsic to being rational

Premise 3. Humans want, in their own self-interest, to be content, to lead a 'right' and 'good', virtuous life.

Premise 4. In their own self-interest they need to consider the interests of others

Premise 5. Therefore humans choose to behave in morally good ways.

The origin of these premises.Premises 1 and 2 and 3 are *a priori* self-evident assumptions. Aristotle may have thought long and hard before he made these *a priori* assumptions but they are the result of his 'reasoning' rather than sense perception. Premise 4 and 5 are based on deductive, standard '*if.....then*' reason. *If* you want to be content *then act* 'morally good'.

Immanuel Kant (1724-1804)

The Categorical Imperative

Immanuel Kant1, a devout Christian, argued there was a straightforward explanation for ethical behaviour. He saw such behaviour as completely objective, transcending all cultures and applying to all rational human beings and having nothing whatsoever to do with any religious beliefs. He explains this 'supreme principle of morality', which he calls the 'categorical imperative' in his introductory book on the nature of morality. What follows is a very simplified account of his theories.

As physical human beings we are controlled by the physical laws of the universe, those laws, which natural scientists explore and define. Controlled by these physical laws we act out of instinct. When we act out of instinct, even if the instinct is positive as it is when we love, this act is not rational. Such instinctive, non-rational action is neither good nor bad, neither

1   *Foundations of the Metaphysics of Morals* 1795

right nor wrong. But, he argues, because we are human we are rational, capable of reason. And because we reason we are aware of our ethical responsibilities, our moral duties to each other and to ourselves. These ethical responsibilities come from our ability as humans to reason, to be rational. When we act, aware of our duty, with rational intention, in a good way, doing what our reason rather than our instinct, tells us to do, then that action is ethically good. The rational guidance we give ourselves to act out of duty is the 'categorical imperative'

An imperative is a command, an instruction that something must be done. Categorical here means absolute. A categorical imperative therefore is something that once our reason tells us it is ethically right; we must do it. Here is Kant's claim, step by step:

Premise 1. Humans are controlled by physical laws of the universe

Premise 2. These laws are beyond our control and are an instinctive

Premise 3. Instincts are not rational

Premise 4. But because we can reason we can overcome our instincts and determine what is morally good and bad.

Premise 5. Once our reason has given us a moral right we must do what that moral right tells us.

This reasoned awareness of good and bad creates the categorical imperative, to act in an ethical way. 'Categorical' here means *absolute* and 'imperative' means *must* be done.

Premise 6. So our ethical behaviour comes from overcoming our natural instincts.

The TOK knowledge issues: Premises 1, 2 and 3 are assumptions, *a priori* assumptions. They may be the result of much hard and difficult thought, but they are the product of Kant's introspective 'reason' rather than empirical, sense perception based, experience. Premise 4 is deductive reason, *if* we can reason *then* we can overcome our instincts. Premise 5 is again an *a priori* assumption, the assumption being that

we act morally when we have to. Premise 6 is an obvious logical outcome if the premises 1 to 5 are true.

Ayn Rand (1905-1982)

Ethical Egoism

Both Aristotle and Kant focus on the well being of the individual as the basis for ethical theory, but a basic idea they have in common is that the ethical way to act assumes a moral duty to other people. They share the assumption that other people's interests must be taken into account. Ayn Rand's adopted ethical philosophy, (she was not the originator, but was a strong proponent) known *asethical egoism,* is founded on the idea that each person ought to pursue his or own self-interest exclusively. We have no moral duty, she claims, than to do what is best for ourselves.

Here is not the place to describe the pros and cons of ethical egoism but Ayn Rand was particularly forceful in putting forward a central argument, which went like this:

Premise 1. A person has only one life to live and this life is therefore of ultimate value to the individual.

Premise 2: Most ethical theories regard our moral duty to help others at the expense of ourselves, to be altruistic.

Premise 3: Therefore these theories do not value the individual.

Premise 4. Ethical egoism is the only moral theory that takes the individual seriously

Premise 5. Ethical egoism should be widely accepted as the doctrine with which we should set our moral standards .

Back to the TOK knowledge issue, from where did Ayn Rand's get her argument? Premise 1 is yet again, *a priori*. She has accepted as an axiom that with only one life to live that life is of ultimate value to the liver. Premise 2 is a reasoned deduction from her awareness of other moral codes and the remaining three premises arise deductively from these two.

Whatever the differences in the ideas behind these theories we can see from a TOK viewpoint all three have something in common. Each one starts with a priori assumptions and then uses deductive logic to establish ethical theories.

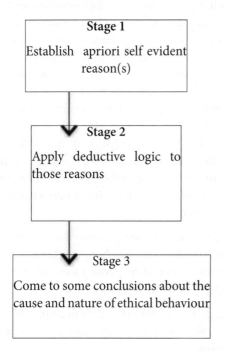

Stage 1, of course, presents the major knowledge issue. Aristotle begins with the assumption that humans are fundamentally rational. Many philosophers dispute this (and so do many psychologists). Kant's first two premises, that humans are controlled by instinctive physical laws and these laws are beyond human control, are also disputable. Rand's assumption too can be rationally queried. A person has only one life, but there are many examples of human endeavour and sacrifice suggesting that many things can be valued above that life.

A priori knowledge has been described as 'non-sensory knowledge of certain propositions acquired by a direct intellectual insight. The kind of knowledge thus obtained has often been labelled 'intuitive knowledge"[2] (Intuition is one of TOK's linking concepts and you can read more about that in Chapter 15).

Perhaps we should end by looking at a model suggested by a contemporary ethicist, Mel Thompson, in his 2009 book *Understand Ethics*. Ethical theorists, he claims, starts by observing the moral choices people make and the reasons they give for them. These theorists then examine the choices and reasons for moral decisions and attempt to create a theory or theories which explain the decisions. They then return to actual moral making situations to see if their theories make sense logically and practically.

This, of course, is rather like human science. Ethicists, observe, collect data, create theories, return to check their theories. But, Thompson claims, ethicists seek to judge behaviour whereas scientists just want to find out what the behaviour is. If Thompson is right modern ethicists not only want to understand moral behaviour, they want control it.

2   Charles Landesman. An introduction to Epistemology Blackwell 1997

Chapter 15

Linking Concepts

TOK diagram implies connections between Knower(s), *Ways of Knowing* and *Areas of Knowledge*. In order to make the connections clearer the TOK curriculum designers introduced into the Curriculum Guide what they called 'linking questions'. To quote the Guide

Connections between the elements of the TOK programme can also be explored through further linking questions … …which raise issues and concepts central to the course.

Eleven 'linking concepts' are listed in the Guide.[1] :

BELIEF

CERTAINTY

CULTURE

EVIDENCE

EXPERIENCE

EXPLANATION

INTERPRETATION

INTUITION

TECHNOLOGY

TRUTH

VALUES

In the Guide each of these headings is followed by a quotation and a series of three to eight questions. These quotations and questions often indicate when specific information is required. Under 'Belief' for instance the fourth out of five questions is.

Does some degree of unjustified belief exist within each element of the TOK diagram?

This question implies that students discussing responses to this question are aware of the significance of the phrase 'unjustified belief' and should be able to put it in the context of Plato's Justified True Belief definition of knowledge.

Under 'Truth' the first out of five questions is

How useful are the truth tests of coherence, correspondence and pragmatism in arriving at knowledge?

Such a questions can only be answered if the students discussing possible answers have an awareness of these three truth tests.

---

1   2008 TOK Guide pages 36-40

The questions also place the eleven concepts in a TOK context. 'Technology' or 'Culture' for instance are words which have a meaning outside of TOK. The questions narrow down their meaning and place them within the framework of TOK. This chapter explores these linking concepts within that framework.

Linking Concept 1:

BELIEF

Philosophers, from the ancient Greeks to the present day, concern themselves with the question: *What can we claim we truly know?* And the follow up question: *How can we separate what we truly know from what we believe?*

These epistemologists, as philosophers who study knowledge are called, have come to an awareness that there are two kinds of belief, *justified belief*, which they claim is certain knowledge and *unjustified belief*, knowledge we cannot be certain off.

Justified Belief

For you to be sure you know something, philosophers claim, for you to have certain knowledge, your knowledge claim has to fulfil three conditions.

- Your knowledge claim has to be true.

- Your knowledge claim must be justified.

- You must believe your knowledge claim.

Example: Knowledge claim:

I know that TOK is a compulsory component of the IB Diploma course

Is this **true**?

The answer is clearly yes. (Truth is also one of the TOK linking concepts).

Can you **justify** this truth?

Again the answer is yes, but *justification* here needs to be understood in a TOK context

True Justification, for our TOK purposes, can be achieved in two main ways: by *reason* and by *sense perception*. (Reason and sense perception are also *Ways of Knowing* in the TOK diagram.)

Justification 1: Reason

The first source of evidence for your being justified in your belief is reason. Reason is the basis of much of our knowledge (See Chapter 4). As a TOK student you need to understand certain things about reason. Think of it now as simply *correct, universally accepted, reasoning*. The kind of reasoning which tells you if you were at school last Friday at 3 p.m. you could not have been at home (Unless, of course, home and school are the same place). All reason is not as simple as this.

Justification 2: Sense perception

The second source of evidence for your being justified in your belief is through your own sense perception.   What your senses perceive, your sense perception, is one of the main sources of your knowledge of the world. Your five main senses are, of course sight, touch, taste, smell and hearing—see Chapter 5.

You might think that the example of the compulsory aspect of TOK is rather superficial. So, try substituting a rather more controversial and personal statement which might be relevant to some of you using this book.

Knowledge claim: *I know that at the end of my twelfth grade I will obtain an IB diploma with at least forty points*

Is this knowledge claim true?

Is it *true* that at the end of my twelfth grade I will obtain an IB diploma with at least forty points? Can you be sure of this? Is there any possible doubt you will get such a Diploma? Is it possible to know the truth about the future?

Can you justify this truth?

Is your belief that you will get a diploma with forty points *justified*? Now, here we have to weigh the evidence. What are your predicted grades? Have you completed all the necessary course work? Are you a conscientious and talented student? Can you really justify the notion that you will get a diploma with at least forty points? Will your justification be through reason and/or sense perception?

Do you believe this knowledge claim?

Do you *believe* that at the end of your twelfth grade you will obtain an IB diploma with at least forty points? If you don't believe this then you cannot know it. It would be ridiculous to claim you know you are going to get a diploma with more than forty points if you really don't believe you are going to.

To what conclusions do these three questions lead you? Test the statement step by step. If you do not believe your claim, if your claim is not true, and if your claim is not justified and you do not believe it, then you do not have knowledge that is justified true belief. So now you have a formula that can be used to test the different kinds of knowledge you meet in the various disciplines you study.

Justified True Belief

Or 'Knowledge'

- Must be justified by reason and/or

  sense perception

- Must be true.

- Must be believed.

The examples of the application of this formula have been chosen to apply to you as a TOK student. In terms of the creation of knowledge by scientists and historians and other scholars the formula is still valid. Astronomers announcing their newly acquired knowledge of a new solar system in deep space must justify their claims by sense perception/empirical evidence and reason and must believe their new knowledge is true. Historians writing the life of Nelson Mandela and analysing his influence on contemporary Africa must give evidence, obtained by perception and reason, to justify the truth of what they believe is his influence.

Unjustified Belief

Unjustified belief, epistemologists argue, is all that belief that cannot be justified by reason or sense perception.

The difference between unjustified believing and knowledge is obvious, you might claim. If you want to believe the sea is made of raspberry juice and all the fish swimming in it are juice drunk fairies, well go ahead and believe. People might be interested in hearing your arguments for believing the sea is raspberry juice but your claim is only that you *believe* it to be raspberry juice, not that it *is* raspberry juice. And providing you don't start collecting it and selling it as genuine raspberry juice, or expecting anyone else to think it is raspberry juice, why shouldn't you believe it? People on the whole are fairly tolerant and provided your belief doesn't harm you or them, why shouldn't you believe what you want to? There is an obvious difference between unjustified belief and knowledge.

Or is there?

Are you quite sure where the boundary is between your knowing something and your believing something? For hundreds of years people 'knew' the world was flat. And we know now that it is approximately spherical. Perhaps a lot of our knowledge is 'flat earth' knowledge and we are unaware of it. Perhaps there are many things we think we 'know' that are unjustified belief.

Knowledge is one of those words that bewitch our intelligences. For many philosophers 'knowledge' is certain and communicable understanding provided by justified true belief. But there are other kinds of knowledge, knowledge by acquaintance, knowledge by faith, by empathy, by introspection, by conscience, by instinct, by intuition. We still call what we know in these ways 'knowledge'; much of this knowledge is created by our Emotions. Emotion is a *Way of Knowing* in the TOK diagram. (See Chapter 6). Emotion may not create justified true belief but it is a very powerful *Way of Knowing*.

Beware then of underestimating the importance of unjustified belief as a way of knowing. What people believe can sometimes be much more important to them than what they know. For many ancient Greeks the belief that gods controlled their destiny was more important than anything else in determining their actions. Even though you think your beliefs are under your control and are a matter of choice, they are often not recognised as beliefs. The Greeks didn't just believe the gods controlled them, they thought they knew, in the same way as people thought they knew the world was flat.

Recent TOK prescribed essay questions included 'What criteria do you use to distinguish between knowledge and opinion?' and 'Discuss the importance of reason and emotion in distinguishing between belief and knowledge?' The implication in these questions seems to be that 'knowledge' is that justified true belief epistemologists wants it to be and that it does not include other kinds of knowledge such as knowledge by acquaintance, conviction or faith. The ambiguity is there for you to explore. As with many words you have to examine 'knowledge' in context to attempt to understand its meaning. If in doubt make clear your understanding of the word, based not on a dictionary definition but your awareness of it in the TOK context.

Linking Concept 2:

CERTAINTY

Certainty is one of those words you know already. If you ask your friend when the next TOK assignment is due and she says 'Monday 29th' and you reply 'Are you certain?' you are asking her if she is absolutely sure of this, if the knowledge she is passing on to you is (a) totally free from error and (b) without doubt.

So it is with 'certainty' in TOK: certainty is knowledge without error and totally free from doubt. Epistemologists of course, can't just leave it at that. They claim there are various kinds of certainty. One of these kinds of certainty is *psychological certainty*, when a person

believes they know something for absolute sure and will never give that belief up regardless of the justification.

The kind of certainty we need to concern ourselves with in TOK is not psychological certainty but knowledge certainty. This is certainty about knowledge that is absolutely indisputable.

Some philosophers, known as Sceptics, claim it is impossible to be certain of anything. These Sceptics hold the view that certain— 'certain' here in the sense of 'undisputable'— knowledge may be sought but will never be found. Sceptics believe you can never be sure of anything.

Absolute sceptics claim that we cannot know anything. Absolute Scepticism would seem to be impossible: if you don't know anything how can you know you don't know anything?

Relative sceptics claim that, well, perhaps we can know something but we must be very careful in our claims to know.

Scepticism may seem strange: it may be obvious to you that you do know certain things so why should anyone suggest or argue that you don't know these things?

Sceptics have three main arguments for their attitude.

- Our senses often deceive us.

Sceptics argue we can never know for certain when we are being deceived by our senses and when we are not. So, if we can't be certain of our sense perception we can't be certain of our knowledge of the external world that we receive through our senses.

- We can never be sure if we are dreaming or not.

Sceptics maintain that we can never be sure whether at any moment we are dreaming or not. If, they claim, you can't be sure you're dreaming then you can't be sure you are experiencing reality either.

Perhaps after all you are not reading these words, you are dreaming that you are reading these words. If we don't know whether we are dreaming or not, how can we be sure of anything?

- Our thoughts are an unreliable interpretation of reality.

Our thoughts are the only things we can really be sure of and our thoughts may be completely different from the reality they attempt to interpret.

The most celebrated argument for scepticism is to be found in Descartes' First Meditation *On Doubt & Certainty*. Like Plato, Descartes wanted to establish what it was possible to be sure of knowing. Before he could begin to undertake this task he believed it essential to free himself from all his existing beliefs because they might be incorrect, and he had no way of knowing whether they were correct or not. Once he had got rid of all his beliefs, he claimed, he could then start to build up a body of knowledge, which was acceptable to him as certain.

René Descartes (1596-1660).

The father of modern philosophy, René Descartes was born in central France in the town of Le Haye, which is now named Descartes in his honour. He studied at a Jesuit College, but was so discontented with the philosophical ideas of the time that were taught there he joined the army of the Duke of Bavaria and travelled widely across Europe. In Bavaria, in the winter of 1619, cooped up in his military billet, he conceived the idea of reconstructing the whole of philosophy anew, with mathematical reasoning as the model of all 'rational' knowledge.

After leaving the army he developed his philosophical ideas in Paris, and later, from 1628, in Holland. As well as developing philosophical 'rationalism' he was the founder of analytical geometry. His most celebrated work is a series of essays, the *Meditations,* published in 1641, the first of which is called *On Doubt and Certainty.* The essays are written in the first person singular - I - and the reader is invited to identify with the 'I' and become personally involved in the arguments.

As well as being known as the creator of the phrase *Cogito, ergo sum*, Descartes is also popularly known for his Method of Cartesian Doubt: treat all your beliefs as if they were false. This, and only this, he argues, will enable you to discover knowledge you can be certain of.

He came up with the idea that he should pretend a cunning evil demon was trying to deceive him; and all the information he was receiving through his senses was created by this evil demon only to deceive him. He would then be able to force himself not to believe the information because it was created by the evil demon.

After taking the sceptical argument to its limit in the First Meditation he establishes, in his Second Meditation, that there is one certainty, the certainty he exists. He exists because he thinks. He argues that even if there is a demon trying to deceive him, he, Descartes, must exist, solely because he is able to think about the demon. His thinking alone was evidence for his existence. His thinking doesn't have to be profound, it just has to be thinking. His body may be the creation of the demon, but his thoughts are not. His thoughts are independent of external things, independent of any sense experience. His thoughts must exist independently of anything the demon could create. Hence the famous 'Cogito, ergo sum', 'I think, therefore I am'.

As an IB Diploma TOK student you will be expected to apply the concept of certainty to the *Ways of Knowing* and *Areas of Knowledge*. You might consider, for instance, in what ways reason and sense perception can or cannot give certainty, or whether certainty is a concept that can be exercised in evaluating the 'truth' in a work of art or a mathematical equation. When you think about questions like these ground your thinking in specific examples from the *Ways of Knowing* and *Areas of Knowledge* in the TOK diagram.

Linking Concept 3:

CULTURE

Culture is one of those words, which bewitches the intellect; you have to put it into context to understand what it means. There are three 'culture' questions in the TOK Guide and the word is used only once in the last six sets of prescribed essay titles. In this context the meaning is clear. *Culture* in the context of TOK means those values, (see page 83)) attitudes and practices shared by communities or groups of people.

The IB mission statement that is printed at the beginning of many of the IB documents makes a clear cultural statement.

IBO mission statement

The International Baccalaureate Organization aims to develop inquiring, knowledgeable and caring young people who help to create a better and more peaceful world through intercultural understanding and respect.

To this end the IBO works with schools, governments and international organizations to develop challenging programmes of international education and rigorous assessment.

These programmes encourage students across the world to become active, compassionate and lifelong learners who understand that other people, with their differences, can also be right.

Does the culture of your school reflect the values in this mission statement? Does the school purposefully and positively develop intercultural understanding and respect? Does it promote the idea that 'other people, with their differences, can also be right?'

The TOK perspective on culture emphasises, of course, the relationship between knowledge and culture, the extent to which different cultures value reason, emotion and the status of say psychology and literature.

As a Knower at the centre of the TOK diagram you should be prepared to consider seriously the values attitudes and practices of your culture in the context of the IB mission statement and in particular your culture's values underpinning the different Areas of Knowledge in the TOK diagram.

Linking Concept 4:

EVIDENCE

You are probably most familiar with the word *evidence* being used in connection with court scenes on television. Evidence is the thing prosecutors place in a plastic bag and label 'Exhibit A'. Exhibit A is brought before the court to demonstrate the truth of a claim.

Evidence in its TOK context is exactly the same, the knowledge that is presented by knower(s) to demonstrate the truth of their claims to know. A fundamental TOK knowledge issue is what is considered evidence in each of the areas of knowledge. In the natural and human sciences and history the evidence is clear. In the sciences the evidence is information obtained by sense perception, by observing the 'phenomena' of the universe. In history the evidence is the primary and secondary sources. The evidence is the objective 'facts' of the scientists and historians, the 'hard' data on which they build their theories. The theories themselves are not evidence. What the knowers use this evidence for is something else. The deductive and inductive reasoning or the imaginative interpretation of the 'knowers' is not evidence.

To understand where history and science evidence comes from is relatively easy. Evidence in the arts is a little more problematic. TOK examines where the artist—the painter or poet or musician- gets the evidence on which his knowledge is based. The answer as suggested in Chapter 13, is that mixture of reason and sense perception and emotion that is individual to the artist. This is clearly quite a different kind of evidence from the objective evidence of the scientist and historian.

Mathematics present a different problem with evidence. Mathematicians agree on the axioms which underpin their discipline and form the basic evidence of mathematics. These axioms come from *a priori* reasoning which hard line empiricists would argue is not evidence at all. The deductive reasoning that mathematicians use in their 'proofs' could also be regarded as evidence, evidence that the mathematical conclusions are correct.

The final TOK area of knowledge, ethics, brings different 'evidence' challenges. Mathematicians agree on their axiom, moral philosophers seem not even to be able to do that. Ethicists are seeking evidence for how we should behave, rather than how we *do* behave. Clearly a different kind of evidence is necessary.

In the TOK context it is helpful to think that evidence can come from the four ways of knowing and that these ways of knowing give access to different kinds of evidence. A wise person i has been claimed by many a lawyer, proportions his belief according to the evidence. One of the things TOK aims to do is to look at the ways of knowing and areas of knowledge and recognise there is much knowledge other than that generated by reason. Understanding the nature of the evidence is a key TOK concept.

Linking Concept 5:

EXPERIENCE

Experience is another of those bewitching words. One of the recent TOK prescribed titles began: *To understand something you have to rely on your own experience and culture.* The meaning of experience here seems straightforward. It means something you have personally encountered, undergone or lived through. If, for instance you have a passionate interest in gorillas and you have read every book and seen every movie and documentary about gorillas you may understand a lot about gorillas but you have not experienced them. You have experienced books and movies and documentaries. If you have trekked up the Ruwenzori Mountains in western Uganda and have spent time personally observing a gorilla family face-to-face, watching their reaction to each other and to your presence, and smelled the distinctive smell of their 'nests', and heard the sounds they make when they warn you keep your distance, then you have experienced gorillas.

If you look at the experience questions in the TOK guide you might be forgiven for thinking this direct personal experience is what TOK experience is about but this might be oversimplifying the knowledge issues embedded in the word 'experience'. The second question in the Guide—What kind of knowledge can be gained through experience?—gets to the heart of TOK. You are now being invited to explore how experience is created in the six areas defined in the TOK diagram. Knowledge obtained by direct observation is knowledge by experience, the kind of knowledge you get when you visit the gorillas. So the sciences and the arts, which begin with observation, sensory perception as the TOK diagram calls it, are those that are experience based. But, of course, there is another kind of experience, the kind of thought experience you have when dealing with abstract concepts like grammatical constructs in language or calculus in maths. Experience can be abstract and rational as well as sense based.

CAS is an important part of the Diploma Programme. The knowledge you acquire through CAS is acquired by experience but it is not the experience alone that makes the knowledge. It is your processing of that experience in a way similar to the way scientists and artists process their experience to construct new knowledge. An important aspect of TOK is making you

aware, as a critical thinking 'knower', how your cultural and value laden 'self' processes experience and makes it your own 'knowledge'.

Linking concept 6:

EXPLANATION

Explanation is, of course, another of those bewitching words. Aristotle for instance defined four different types of explanation

For TOK purposes the concept of explanation is rooted in the different *Ways of Knowing* and *Areas of Knowledge*. An 'explanation' is that which produces understanding how or why something is as it is. One recently prescribed essay, for instance, invited students to compare how historians and scientists explain something and if explanation in these two disciplines meant the same thing. One of the questions under the heading 'Explanation' in the curriculum guide directly asks what characteristics must an explanation have to be considered good within the different *Ways of Knowing* and *Areas of Knowledge*.

'Explanation' therefore is at the heart of TOK. What academic knowers and artists do is to explain the phenomena of the world about them. As we have seen in earlier parts of this book different disciplines use *Ways of Knowing* in different ways. But all the disciplines attempt to explain. The processes used by natural scientists to explain the phenomena of the physical world use *Ways of Knowing* differently from the mathematicians explaining their Area of Knowledge. When you understand the processes of the construction of knowledge in different disciplines then you understand that 'explanation' differs in TOK's *Areas of Knowledge*.

Linking Concept 7:

INTERPRETATION

Interpretation in its everyday sense means offering an explanation and is therefore closely related in meaning to the previous linking concept.

Within the context of TOK, 'interpretation' must be related to *Ways of Knowing* and *Areas of Knowledge*. The linking questions in the Curriculum Guide make this quite clear. One question opens with a challenge to explore how interpretation occurs within *Areas of Knowledge* and then goes on to ask if some *Ways of Knowing* are less open to interpretation than others. A prescribed essay question (2007) indicated the same understanding of the concept of explanation by asking if some *Ways of Knowing* are less open to interpretation than others.

The knowledge issue implicit in these questions is the *constancy* of the knowledge generated. The Knower(s) having assembled the data, or the evidence, examines alternative interpretations of these data/evidence until they arrive at what they consider the most, perhaps the only, sound explanation. In the sciences, natural and human, there is often little room for interpretation: the 'facts' point the way clearly to a theory. In history, as you have seen, interpretation is an important part of the process of creating new knowledge. Historians interpret and evaluate the evidence. In the arts we are often challenged to interpret. There may be several interpretations of a work of art, all of which may have some validity but it can also be claimed that there is only one valid interpretation. For example, one theory of interpretation in art calls for the viewer or reader to identify what it is the artist intended to accomplish, interpreting the art accordingly and asking the question, *To what extent has the artist accomplished this aim?*

One of the aims of TOK is to get you, the student, to critically consider such issues across the *Ways of Knowing* and *Areas of Knowledge*. In general the less open knowledge is to interpretation the firmer should be our trust in that knowledge.

Linking Concept 8:
INTUITION

Much has been written by epistemologists, those philosophers who study the nature of knowledge and knowing, and more recently psychologists, about *intuition*.

Epistemologists have labelled *a priori* knowledge, the knowledge for instance that creates axioms in mathematics, *intuitive knowledge*. This intuitive knowledge is knowledge which is not based on sensory perception but which comes from an alternative intellectual insight. This is obviously a specialised use of the word but one which TOK students should be aware. In ethics, as well as mathematics, intuitive knowledge of epistemologists it has been argued, underpins significant ideas in those disciplines and has no sensory justification.

This intuitive knowledge of epistemologists is not the same as the *intuition* that is the study of psychologists. Psychologists see *intuition* in its more popular understanding as ideas and thoughts that come to mind quickly and without much reflection.

The questions in the TOK curriculum guide and the prescribed essay are concerned with the psychologists' definition of the word rather than the epistemologists'. One question in the guide specifically refers to 'what is commonly called "intuition"' and another quotes Germaine Greer as referring to "the frequently celebrated female intuition", indicating that the word *intuition* is used in TOK in its more popular meaning rather than the technical way that epistemologists might use. Any student attempting an essay presentation centring on the word *intuition* would be wise to consider carefully the relationship between *a priori* knowledge and intuitional knowledge before dismissing a philosophical interpretation of the word.

The fundamental TOK intuition questions must be about what part intuition plays in *Ways of Knowing* and the different *Areas of Knowledge*. There are many examples of knowledge created apparently by intuition that on close scrutiny are not really intuitive at all, but the result of a well prepared mind suddenly coming upon an understanding. Einstein for instance claims that his basic insight into the relativity of time came to him one morning just as he got out of bed but added that this moment of truth—of intuition some might call it—had been preceded by ten years of thinking about the subject.

Intuition certainly has a role in the creation of certain kinds of knowledge but any claims to be taken seriously must be carefully examined case by case.

Linking Concept 9:

TECHNOLOGY

A prescribed essay title which was by far the most popular of its year (2006) was 'Can a machine know?'. The examiner's comments on this essay take you right to the heart of TOK: 'The intention behind this question was to explore what we mean by "knowledge" in different contexts - and essays structured by *Areas of Knowledge* or *Ways of Knowing*, tend to retain this focus.'

When you consider technology in a TOK context have in your mind the TOK diagram. Consider how technology can influence or change the *Ways of Knowing* and how this affects the knowledge, which is created and how we value that knowledge.

An obvious way in which technology affects the expansion of knowledge is through its ability to expand our *sense perception*. Radio telescopes can 'see' further into outer space, 'colliders' can show us what happens to matter in extreme conditions, carbon dating can give precise time patterns, DNA can indicate migrations that took place thousands of years ago. Computers can also *reason* with a speed and accuracy that even ten years ago was impossible.

Technology has also revolutionised communication. At the press of a button or two we have access to unlimited amounts of information and data and the 'knowledge' this information and data imply. A major knowledge issue for TOK is where this information and data comes from and its 'truth' or reliability. The *language* of computers can cross-conventional linguistic barriers and perhaps influence the way we use language to develop ideas or even to 'think'.

Perhaps the Way of Knowing least affected by technology is *emotion*. But even in claiming this in TOK terms it is necessary to establish why machines do not have emotions and what kinds of 'knowledge' might therefore be inaccessible to machines.

Linking Concept 10:

TRUTH

The 'word' truth appears frequently in the prescribed titles. Usually the student is asked to compare truth in different *Ways of Knowing* and *Areas of Knowledge*. Typically such a question would ask directly for a comparison: *are some Ways of Knowing more likely to lead to the truth than others*? The knowledge issues here are clearly those which touch on the way the knowledge is created, how truth can be different for instance, in history and maths or art. Similar questions include a quote from Picasso: *Art is a lie that brings us nearer to the truth*, which students are invited to discuss relative to a particular branch of art.

Other questions are more specifically related to the concept of truth itself although students will still be expected to illustrate their ideas through *Areas of Knowledge* and *Ways of Knowing*. One question asks how can *Ways of Knowing* help us to distinguish between something that is true and something that is believed to be true, concentrating on the *Ways of Knowing* rather than the *Areas of Knowledge*.

For TOK you should certainly be familiar with certain basic ideas of truth: Plato's concept of truth, of the ideas of absolute and relative truth and of three (of the many) theories of truth philosophers have developed over the years.

Plato's Truth

According to Plato (See Linking concept 1, Belief), anything less than justified true belief cannot be knowledge. His first condition of justified true belief is that knowledge must be true. Truth for Plato, has three characteristics: it has to be public, it has to be independent and it has to be eternal.

Plato's Truth 1: *Truth is public*

Truth is public. Truth is true for everybody. You cannot say 'What is true for me is true for me and what is true for you is true for you'. No matter how strongly you believe your watch keeps time perfectly if it does not keep time perfectly your belief is not true: you cannot, truthfully, claim your watch keeps time perfectly. You could, truthfully claim that your belief is it keeps time perfectly. But that is a different truth. That is a truth about your belief. There are two truths here.

- Your watch keeps time perfectly

- Your belief that your watch keeps time perfectly. .

Both of these statements are true both for you and everyone else.

Plato's Truth 2: *Truth is independent*

Truth is independent of anyone's beliefs. The truth of the statement 'Your watch keeps time perfectly' is independent of whether you think it is true or not. You could persuade all your friends that your watch keeps time perfectly; indeed you could persuade the entire world your watch keeps time perfectly, but that doesn't mean your watch keeps time perfectly. The statement can be false even though everyone you know, indeed everyone in the world, believes it to be true.

Plato's Truth 3: *Truth is eternal*

Truth is eternal. Now here we have a slight problem with your watch. It might be that as your watch gets older it no longer keeps time perfectly (if it ever did). But the current proposition, *your watch keeps time perfectly* (if it does) is true for now and will be true for now forever. If your watch changes, the truth that it once kept perfect time will not change. Truth is not a watch.

This simple, many would say too simple, definition of truth is a very limited definition. Much philosophical thinking has taken place since Plato's day and his definition of truth is now considered a little naïve.

Absolute Truth and Relative Truth

Plato saw truth as absolute. He was quite clear on this: you must be absolutely certain before you claim to know the truth. Truth for him, and many later philosophers, is a straightforward, simple matter: plain objective fact, transparent and open, empirically and logically proven. It describes objective and rational reality.

Other philosophers claim there is no such thing as absolute truth. All truth is relative, they argue. For them nothing is plain or objective, there is no one truth, there is no one reality. Reality is different for each of us, people and different groups of people have different understandings of reality. Truth for you is different from truth for me. The greatest relativist of them all, Nietzsche, wrote 'There are no facts, only interpretations'.

Absolute truth

This seems the common sense approach. Truth is what really is out there. Reality is objective. It does not depend on what we think it to be. The room you are sitting in now either has a door or doesn't have a door. You went to school this morning on foot, in a car, on the train, by some other method of transport or a combination of all those methods.

Relative truth.

Relativists claim everything is subject to human interpretation. We are forced, they argue, whether we want to, or not, to see the world from our own partial and therefore restricted perspectives. Simply put, your understanding of the physical circumstances you are now in is a different understanding from anyone else's. Anna, who is sitting opposite you in the room, perceives the room quite differently from you or anyone else. Anna's interpretation of reality, her truth, is quite different from yours.

That example is about a physical 'truth'. Consider an ethical example: Anna has asked you to help her with her final TOK essay, the one that she has to sign as being all her own work.

She wants to discuss some ideas with you. How much help can you give? She says you can give unlimited help because in the end it is she who writes the essay and it will be her work. Is there a clear-cut line between her work and what she makes of your reaction to her ideas? Where is the truth?

Relativist tools: Language, culture and experience.

Relativists insist there are many different ways of understanding the world and none of them really reflect the Way Things Really Are. We understand the world, they claim, by inquiring into it and reaching an understanding of it. That understanding is our 'truth'. There are many different ways of making that inquiry and the tools we use influence the 'truth' we arrive at. The tools we use to make our inquiry, our language, our culture and our experience, they argue, make truth relative, absolute truth is unattainable.

Over the centuries philosophers debated the nature of truth and developed many 'theories' about it. Three of these theories are mentioned in the Curriculum Guide: the Correspondence Theory, the Coherence Theory and the Pragmatic Theory.

The Correspondence Theory

Plato and his Athenian friends were the first to formulate this theory and it is still the most easily understood and accepted theory of truth.

Truth, according to this theory, *is what propositions have when they correspond to reality.* (Note it is the proposition that is true, not the reality).

Put simply:

For any proposition (p) — p is true if, and only if, p corresponds to the facts.

So here is a proposition : *Bishkek is the capital city of Kyrgyzstan.*

This proposition is only true if Bishkek is the capital city of Kyrgyzstan.

A closer to home example (unless you live in Bishkek) is a proposition based on the belief that all TOK students arrive punctually for class.

Here is the proposition: *All TOK students arrive punctually for class.*

That is true if, and only if, all TOK students really do arrive punctually for class. If they are all in class when the class is due to start the truth of my proposition, according to the Correspondence Theory, is established. The proposition is true because it corresponds to the facts.

The Coherence Theory

The Correspondence Theory claims you have truth when a proposition corresponds to reality. The Coherence Theories (there are a lot of them) claim *you have truth when a proposition is compatible with other propositions you accept as established truth.* When all your established truths cohere, when no truth contradicts another truth, then you have it.

Here is an example. Anna's mother wakes her up an hour earlier than normal and tells her not to use the bathroom she normally uses because there is a python in there which has come in during the night through the toilet waste pipe and she (the mother) is waiting for the health authorities to send someone to take it away. Using the Coherence Theory (probably without consciously knowing she is) Anna assesses the proposition *There is a python in the bathroom that has come in through the toilet waste pipe.* She does this by rapidly reviewing what other beliefs she accepts as true which cohere, or not, with the proposition. These might include:

- Pythons can't enter bathrooms through waste pipes

- The area she lives in is not an area where pythons live

- There is not a zoo, or snake park, near her from which it could have escaped

- Her mother would be panicking it there really was a python in the apartment

And most of all,

- Her mother thinks she should get up earlier than she habitually does.

So her mother's proposition fails to cohere with many other things she has good reason to believe are true, so knowing it is not April 1st Anna somewhat bluntly tells her mother to shut the door and go away.

With the *All TOK students arrive punctually for class* proposition, what cohering propositions might allow this as true?

- All TOK students are conscientious and reliable

- They love coming to the TOK class

- The class is never the first class of the day, so there is no problem with arriving late at school

- They are reliably punctual for all other classes

- They hand in their assignments on time

Coherence theory, to summarise, states that a proposition is true if it is consistent with other established truths.

The Pragmatic Theory

The Pragmatic Theory of Truth is based on the ideas of American Philosopher, Charles Sanders Peirce (1839-1914). His Pragmatic Theory claims that a proposition is true if it is useful to believe. Beliefs that are most useful to us, beliefs that are the best justification for the things we do, beliefs that promote success, are truths. Truth is proved, or disproved, by our subjective experience.

Let's stay with Anna. She also believes that she is surrounded by people who love and care for her. So the pragmatists say her proposition *I am surrounded by people who love and care for me* is true if she finds it useful. Her belief justifies what she does and promotes success for her. Until such time as she finds, through her

subjective experience, that the proposition is not useful, it will be true, for her.

Examine the proposition *All TOK students arrive punctually for class* through the lens of the Pragmatic Theory and what do you get? The Theory says the proposition is true if it is useful to believe. It is useful for the teacher to believe if the teacher wants the students to be punctual. If they are not punctual, and the teacher still believes they are, where does that leave the truth? Is it useful for the teacher to believe students arrive punctually even when they do not? The pragmatists would say, you have to be pragmatic. If it is useful for the teacher to believe students arrive on time, then the teacher must, pragmatically accept that they do arrive on time. If it is useful for the students to believe the truth is they arrive on time, then they arrive on time. Our beliefs promote success. Pierce would say they enable us to predict experience.

Truth and TOK

Whatever your own ideas are about the nature of truth, TOK truth is best put in the context of *Areas of Knowledge* and *Ways of Knowing*. You must come to your own conclusions about the nature of truth in the Areas and Ways and you can only do that if you have a good critical awareness of the way knowledge is constructed in those Areas and Ways. You must also come to some awareness of what, for you, in the TOK context, is truth. You may come to the conclusion that different *Areas of Knowledge* use different theories of truth, or perhaps a mixture of all three theories. You may decide that absolute truth is the standard by which knowledge must be judged and relative truth is simply a compromise.

Linking Concept 11: VALUES

Even it we come from the same country and go to the same school and take the same IB Diploma subjects we each have our own unique culture and our own sense of what is important, our own values. The circumstances in which we were brought up, our age, our race, our gender, the languages we speak, our religious beliefs and many, other things influence us. Our values determine what we believe is good or bad and how we should treat other people. Much of your interpretation of what is acceptable ethical behaviour will depend on your personal values.

Values too are often shared with the people we live and work with, and are cultural. Think for a moment of the values of your own school. Is academic success valued more than sporting prowess? What groups of students do other students hold in high esteem? By teachers? Is there anything about your school, which makes you and your students proud to be part of the school? Answering these question will help you understand your shared cultural values.

Knowers, in the TOK context, can be expected to have their own values. Mathematicians can have a shared set of values, as can historians, and an obvious TOK knowledge issue would be to what extent these values overlap. The TOK Curriculum Guide and prescribed essay questions approach values from two opposing perspectives. They mainly ask how values influence, and are used in, the different *Ways of Knowing* and *Areas of Knowledge*, inviting students to consider, for instance, what and why certain research is undertaken by Knowers and what values they bring to their work. But the questions also invite students to consider what values are implicit in *Ways of Knowing* and *Areas of Knowledge* and to explore the ways in which they influence the way we think and act.

Chapter 16

Assessment

Three Diploma Points

Along with CAS and the Extended Essay, TOK is a compulsory part of the IB Diploma. If you do not submit a TOK Essay and a TOK Presentation of acceptable quality you will not be awarded a diploma.

The maximum you can score on the TOK Essay is 40 and on the Presentation, 20, making a total of 60. These points are then converted into grades as follows:

48-60 A

38-47 B

29-37 C

19-28 D

0- 18 E

Similar grades A to E are also awarded for the Extended Essay. IB examiners use the grades for both TOK and the Extended Essay to award a maximum of three diploma points. If students score an A in both TOK and the Extended Essay or one A (TOK or Extended Essay) and one B(TOK or Extended Essay) they score 3 points. If they score two Bs and a combination of at least one A with a C or D they score 2 points; a combination of C and D is awarded 1 point. If both scores are D no points are given but a diploma can still be awarded.

An A grade in either TOK or the Extended Essay earns a point even if the other grade is an E. But if one of the grades, either TOK or the Extended Essay, is an E you must achieve a minimum of 28 points to be eligible for a diploma. An E grade in *both* TOK and the Extended Essay is an automatic failure.

The Essay

The TOK Essay and Presentation are graded according to criteria detailed in the Curriculum Guide. Before you begin to prepare either the Essay or the Presentation you should look carefully at these criteria.

The Essay is marked on 4 criteria each of which has a maximum of 10, giving a total of 40. You will notice that two of the criteria, A and C, are specifically about 'knowledge issues' and the second criterion again emphasises knowledge issues 'connected to the student's own learning'.

The essay titles are designed to reflect the TOK diagram. Examine any list of prescribed titles and you will see that many of them refer directly to Ways of Knowing and Areas of Knowledge. A typical questions might be *When should we trust our senses to give us truth ?* (May 2009) Obviously what is expected here is to look at a Way of Knowing (sense perception) and to explore the nature of the truth, a linking concept, it can generate), and then to select at least two Areas of Knowledge in which the sense perception 'truth' either does, or does not use the generated knowledge.

The Presentation

The Presentation is also marked on 4 criteria each of which has a maximum of 5 points, giving a total of 20. You will notice Criteria A and B are specifically about knowledge issues. As part of the presentation you also have to complete a form in which you describe the planning for your presentation and you must define—to use the words of the form— 'the knowledge issue that will be the focus of your presentation'.

The Annual TOK Subject Report

Each year, usually sometime in April or May, the IB's Chief Examiner for TOK issues a report discussing the standard of the previous year's essays and presentations. The report describes what was done well and what improvements could take place. Before you write your essay or make your presentation you *must* read the TOK Examiner's Subject Report for the previous year. In the Report each essay title prescribed for the previous year is reported on individually and examples of knowledge issues given. For instance, the examples of knowledge issues given for the essay question above *When should we trust our senses to give us truth?*

To what extent do our senses give us truth?

To what extent do reason, emotion, language (and other factors) affect our sense perception?

What is the scope, and what are the limits of sensory information in different areas of knowledge? The report on this title ends with listing three ways in which 'stronger students' structured their essays. Stronger students, it states,[1]

- look at how sense perception works in conjunction with other ways of knowing

- see the strengths and weaknesses in contrasting *Areas of Knowledge* (science and religion were common here)

- use a narrative thread. In the most sophisticated essays this was something directly related to perception itself; so, for example, facts that were 'true' in relation to the outside world, and those that were 'true' in relation to aspects of the human, inner world. In these cases the concept of truth was often subject to penetrating analysis.

Information on the Presentation is also given in the Report. The central importance of identifying the knowledge issues arising from a real life situation is emphasised and examples given. For example the real life situation that was the subject of one presentation was considering the issues created by President Ahmadinejad of Iran calling for a conference to establish whether the Jewish Holocaust really happened and one knowledge issue was clearly *How can we draw a clear line between fact and interpretation in history?*

The Examiner's Annual Subject Report is perhaps the most important TOK source available to you. Reading the report carefully is the most useful possible preparation for your essay and presentation. It is available from the IB on line curriculum website.

50 Excellent Theory of Knowledge Essays

Another resource you should use is the IB's CD, *50 Excellent Theory of Knowledge Essays*, a collection of high scoring essays showing a variety of approaches you can use to write a high scoring essay.

---

1   TOK Subject Report 2009 page 4

Bibliography

Chapter 1. Origins

IBO Diploma Programme TOK Guide (First Examination 2008) International Baccalaureate Organisation. March 2006.

Schools Across Frontiers. Second edition. A.D.C.Petersen. Open Court. 1987.

Chapter 2. The TOK Diagram

IBO Diploma Programme TOK Guide (First Examination 2008). International Baccalaureate Organisation. March 2006.

List of TOK prescribed titles for 2012. On line document, International Baccalaureate Organisation. 2010.

Chapter 3. Knowledge Issues

IBO Diploma Programme TOK Guide (First Examination 2008). International Baccalaureate Organisation. 2006.

Understanding Knowledge Issues. On line curriculum document. International Baccalaureate Organisation 2009.

TOK Examiner's Report. On line document. International Baccalaureate Organisation May 2009

Chapter 4. Reason

The Limits of Logic . Aiden Seery. An unpublished lecture given at Munich International School. 1998.

Chapter 5. Sense Perception

Quotations from:

The Marriage of Heaven and Hell. William Blake 1790-93.

The Essential Writings of Ralph Waldo Emerson. Modern Library. 2000.

Zur Farbenlehre. Wolfgang von Goethe. 1810.

De Rerum Natura. Titus Lucretius Carus. 94-55 BC.

Le Petit Prince. Antoine de Saint-Exupéry. 1943.

Ecce Homo. Friedrich Nietzsche. 1888.

Man is the Measure. Reuben Abel. The Free Press.1976.

Essays in Science . Albert Einstein. Philosophical Library. 1934.

Language, Thought and Reality. Benjamin Whorf. MIT. Press 1972.

Human Destiny. Lecomte de Nouy. Longmans Green.1947.

Chapter 6. Emotion

The New Shorter English Dictionary. Oxford University Press.1993.

Emotional Awareness. Paul Ekman. Times Books. 2008.

The Philosophy of Bertrand Russell. Ed. by P.A. Schilp. Library of Living Philosophers. 1946

Chapter 7. Language

The New Shorter English Dictionary. Oxford University Press.1993.

Philosophical Investigations. Ludwig Wittgenstein. Blackwell. 1953.

Thought and Language. Lev Semyonovich Vygotsky. 1934.

American Mythologies. Marshall Blonsky. Oxford University Press USA. 2000.

Poems of Gerard Manley Hopkins. Gerard Manley Hopkins. 1918.

Chapter 8 Faith

IBO Diploma Programme TOK Guide (First Examination 2008) International Baccalaureate Organisation. March 2006.

Callista. John Henry Newman. 1885.

Chapter 9. Natural Science

The Logic of Scientific Discovery. Karl Popper. 1934. Routledge English Edition 1959.

The Structure of Scientific Revolutions. Thomas Kuhn. University of Chicago Press, 1962.

Chapter 10. Mathematics.

The Elements. Euclid. Translated by T.L Heath. Dover 1956.

Zermelo-Frankel Set Theory. Wikipedia website:en.wikipedia.org/wiki/Zermelo-Frankel_set_theory. 2011.

Peano Postulates. Guiseppe Peano. Wikipedia website: en.wikipedia.org/wiki/Guiseppe_Peano. 2011.

The Philosophy of Bertrand Russell. Ed. by P.A. Schilp. Library of Living Philosophers. 1946.

Chapter 11. Human Science

The Hawthorne Effect. Website. Wikipedia. 2011.

Chapter 12. History.

von Ranke. Quoted in *What is History?* by E. H. Carr. Penguin.1961.

The History of the Decline and Fall of the Roman Empire. Edward Gibbon. 1776.

Commentarri de Bello Gallico. Commentaries on the Gallic Wars. Julius Caesar. 50-40 BC.

Huckleberry Finn. Mark Twain. 1885.

Chapter 13. The Arts

What is Art? Leo Tolstoy 1898 . Translated by Almyer Maude. MacMillan. 1960

Education Through Art. Herbert Read. 1954.

Refugee Mother and Child. Chinua Achebe. In *Touched With Fire* Cambridge University Press. 1985.

Huckleberry Finn. Mark Twain. 1885.

The Closing of the American Mind. Allan Bloom. Simon and Schuster.1987.

Chapter 14. Ethics.

The Ethics of Aristotle. Translated by J.A.K. Thomson. Penguin.1976.

Foundations of the Metaphysics of Morals. Immanuel Kant. 1785.

Atlas Shrugged. Ayn Rand. Random House 1957.

An Introduction to Epistemology. Charles Landesman. Blackwell.1997.

Chapter 15. Linking Concepts.

Truth. Stanford Encyclopaedia of Philosophy-Website: plato/stanford.edu/emtries/truth.

Epistemology: Wikipedia. Website: en.wikipedia.org/wiki/Epistemolgy

Meditations on First Philosophy. Rene Descartes. 1641.

IBO Diploma Programme TOK Guide (First Examination 2008). International Baccalaureate Organisation. March 2006.

Chapter16. Assessment

IBO Diploma Programme TOK Guide (First Examination 2008). International Baccalaureate Organisation. 2006.

TOK Examiner's Report. International Baccalaureate Organisation May 2009.

50 Excellent Theory of Knowledge Essays. International Baccalaureate Organisation 2010.

Index